W9-BLJ-338

CHATELAINE
home decor
GARDEN ROOMS

CHATELAINE
home decor

GARDEN ROOMS

Nature-inspired decorating indoors and out

BY JOAN MACKIE

M&S

A SMITH SHERMAN BOOK
produced in conjunction with CHATELAINE®
and published by McCLELLAND & STEWART INC.

© 1998 Maclean Hunter Publishing Limited and Smith Sherman Books Inc.

All rights reserved. No part of this publication may be reproduced, stored in a retrieval system, or transmitted in any form or by any means, electronic, mechanical, photocopying, recording or otherwise, without prior permission of the publishers. For information address McClelland & Stewart Inc., 481 University Avenue, Suite 900, Toronto, Ontario, Canada M5G 2E9.

Canadian Cataloguing in Publication Data

Mackie, Joan

  Garden rooms : nature inspired decorating indoors and out

(Chatelaine home decor)
"A Smith Sherman book produced in conjunction with Chatelaine"
Includes index.

ISBN 0-7710-2008-2

1. Interior decoration. 2. Decoration and ornament – Plant forms.
I. Title. II. Series.

NK2115.M324 1998   747   C98-930400-0

ACKNOWLEDGEMENTS

A BOOK IS NOT simply the outcome of one person toiling alone: many people contribute to the end result. In my case, I have been fortunate to have worked with so many talented people that to name them all with the credit they deserve would require its own chapter. Yet it is these creative people — homeowners, designers, artisans, tradespeople and crafts persons — whose work made this book possible, and I thank them for allowing me to reproduce it.

I also warmly thank Carol Sherman and Andrew Smith of Smith Sherman Books. *Garden Rooms* would never have happened without their vision and creativity; they conceived the idea and then put it all together.

I am grateful to CHATELAINE Editor Rona Maynard for having faith in me to produce exciting decorating features every month, and publisher Lee Simpson for her interest and support. I have also had the privilege of developing ideas with CHATELAINE's art director, Caren Watkins, associate art director, Ann Shier, and creative associate, Barbara Glaser.

Of course, my efforts would be wasted if they were not photographed in the best light possible. So my thanks to photographers, Ted Yarwood and Evan Dion, two of the best in the business.

Also thanks to Bernice Eisenstein for her impeccable attention to detail, Joseph Gisini for his creative input, Erik Tanner, who was always willing to lend an eye, and everyone at McClelland & Stewart.

Finally, I am grateful to my husband, Keith Wagland, for supporting me in all my endeavors.

JOAN MACKIE

COVER PHOTO: *see page 26*

PHOTO PAGE 2: *see page 42*

CREDITS: *see page 127*

PRINTED AND BOUND IN CANADA

CONTENTS

INTRODUCTION 8

INDOOR ROOMS 10

ENTRANCES

PLEASE COME IN 12

   DO-IT-YOURSELF PROJECTS 18–21

      FRAGRANT POTPOURRI
      Turn a blossom-filled garden into bowls of scented petals.

      PANSY BALLS
      Dry pansies for colorful accents.

      TURNING OVER A NEW LEAF
      Give a plain-Jane mirror a makeover.

LIVING ROOMS

ROOMS TO RELAX IN 22

   DO-IT-YOURSELF PROJECTS 32–41

      BLOSSOMING BULBS
      Learn how to "force" bulbs.

      FIT TO BE TILED
      Transform a tired wooden table.

      SHEER GENIUS
      Use sheer fabric to make stylish sophisticated curtains.

      MATERIAL GAINS
      Put traditional floral faces on plain, everyday cushions.

      GOOD CHEMISTRY
      Make innovative flower holders from laboratory glassware.

      GILDED SHADE
      Get a glow on a lampshade with stamped-on paint.

      SNAPPY SCRAP CUSHIONS
      Sew cushion covers with patchwork pieces.

      BLIND AMBITION
      Give a decorator look to an inexpensive window blind.

      HANG UPS
      Make a stunning wall decoration with découpage plates.

      ARMCHAIR FARMING
      Plant a crop for almost-instant indoor greenery.

continued on next page

DINING ROOMS & KITCHENS

FEASTS FOR THE EYES **42**

DO-IT-YOURSELF PROJECTS **50–57**

BASKET CASE
Make a casual centrepiece with a basket filled with flowers.

HERB APPEAL
Perk up windowsills all year long.

FENCED IN
Corral your favorite plants in a fenced-in planter.

SWITCHED ON
Lighten a room with garden-gorgeous switch plates.

LIGHTEN UP
Use a pattern to make your own candle shades.

SERVIETTES WITH STYLE
Stamp your personality on handmade napkins.

ON THE FLOOR FRONT
Stencil a floor rug on a plain wood floor.

LEMON AID
Create simple table decorations with a fruity theme.

TABLE DRESSING
Quilt pretty placemats using floral fabric.

KEEPING TABS
Embellish windows with tab top curtains.

BEDROOMS & BATHROOMS

PERSONAL SPACES, PRIVATE RETREATS **58**

DO-IT-YOURSELF PROJECTS **70–79**

LATTICE LEAF
Build a lattice headboard in under an hour.

PICKET LINE
Create an easy-to-make picket-fence headboard.

BLOOMIN' BEAUTIFUL
Pretty up cushions with a floral print.

TRAY CHIC
Cover a plain tray with fancy fabric.

A STITCH IN TIME
Frame an heirloom embroidery and bring it to life.

FOOLED YOU!
Paint a trompe l'oeil scene.

NO-SEW BILLOWY CURTAINS
Hang sheer curtains, handkerchief style.

WARDROBE WIZARDRY
Protect your clothes stylishly with fabric covers.

FLOWER-POWER WINDOWS
Découpage a plain rod and rings.

COVER UP
Transform storage boxes with fabric.

FLOORED WITH FABULOUS FABRIC
Cover floors and walls with heavyweight cotton fabric.

WINDOW DRESSING
Put a new spin on sheers with printed fabrics.

OUTDOOR ROOMS 80

FRESH-AIR LIVING
GORGEOUS LIVING-ROOM GARDENS 82

DO-IT-YOURSELF PROJECTS 98–105

PAINTING A NEW CANVAS
Use paint and fabric to renovate a canvas chair.

MUSKOKA CHAIR MAKEOVER
Pretty up a plain Muskoka chair with a stencil.

RUSTIC GARDEN BENCH
Make a twig or "tree" bench, ideal for a garden room.

WINDOW BOX
Make a simple but elegant window box.

CONTAINER GARDENING
Fill your garden, patio or deck with pots of plants year round.

DINING ALFRESCO
GOING OUT FOR DINNER 106

DO-IT-YOURSELF PROJECTS 116–123

NOVEL NAPKING RINGS
Make outdoor-inspired napkin rings.

WALL HANGING
Put color on outdoor walls with hanging baskets.

WEIGHTY SUBJECTS
Make decorative weights to anchor outdoor tablecloths.

GARDEN TRELLIS
Build a trellis to define your garden rooms.

PICNIC TABLE PERK UP
Turn a hardware-store basic into a backyard beauty.

GLASS ACTS
Decorate a plain hurricane lamp shade with glass etching.

VINES GROW UP
Grow vines to dress up a yard or balcony.

INDEX 124
CREDITS 127

INTRODUCTION

*I*T IS NATURAL to search for inspiration when decorating a house or apartment — inspiration for a style, a "look," a color palette or theme. Well, what greater muse to excite the imagination than the garden? Here nature presents imagery that gives life to wallpaper, lamps, carpets and fabrics.

Creating a garden room is easy when you base your decorating plans on the elements that already exist in nature. Your color palette might come from the drifts of soft shades that swirl through a perennial border or the brilliance of several fiery hot-colored flowers growing close together. Or the subtle shades of green that distinguish the leaves of one plant, shrub or tree from another. An abundance of options is available, but one thing is certain: nature provides a color to suit everyone's taste.

Garden-inspired decorating gives a room a relaxed and warm feeling. It may be something as simple as the way light plays off a petal in a vase of flowers or a subtle breeze blows through sheer curtains, revealing a glimpse of trees outside. Perhaps it's a pale fern-leaf pattern stencilled on a wall or pots of herbs lined up on a windowsill. Rooms decorated with touches like these embrace you and make you feel instantly welcomed.

They're neither stuffy nor overdecorated, neither precious nor pretentious. When you "walk" into the rooms presented in *Garden Rooms*, you're sure to feel at home. That's what successful decorating is all about.

Garden Rooms is divided into two sections — "Indoor Rooms" and "Outdoor Rooms." In "Indoor Rooms," you'll find exciting garden-inspired examples for every room in the house: entranceways, living and dining rooms, kitchens, bedrooms and baths. In "Outdoor Rooms," the focus is on living and dining, whether it's on the veranda, deck, a high-rise balcony or rooftop. Included throughout the book are more than 50 do-it-yourself projects guaranteed to add that garden-room quality to any room in your house — indoors or out.

Yes, *Garden Rooms* is about floral cushions, botanical prints and pots of flowers. But it's also about magic and mood, romance and warmth and how to achieve all those qualities in your home.

So, settle down for a pleasurable read and a meandering trip through some beautiful rooms, then get out your tape measures, paintbrushes and imagination. You're about to be inspired.

INDOOR

ROOMS

ALFRESCO INSPIRATION

Garden furniture moves indoors, forming a cozy dining area at the end of a large room. A sculptural bird bath with a cherry-wood top looks perfectly at home inside. Tucking up to it, a curved concrete garden bench seats two; patterned floral chintz pretties up a pair of chairs and a two-seater pine settee. A brass chandelier decorated with miniature metal flowers and leaves casts lacy shadows at night.

Entrances
PLEASE COME IN

AN ENTRANCE is like an invitation. Warmly and hospitably inviting you and your guests to enter, it is the welcoming mat of your home. Often small, the entrance merits decorating with as much — if not more — care and flair as every other room.

The entrance is the first impression anyone — including yourself — has of your home; it's where the seeds of your decorating ideas pave the way for the pleasures that await in the rest of the house. Is your home dramatic and formal? Laid back and casual? Pared down and minimalist? Then decorate your entrance with that in mind: it establishes the overall tone and draws you further in.

Bridging the space between indoors and out, an entrance is the ideal area to decorate with a bit of both: perhaps indoor furniture and vases of fragrant flowers cut from the garden; or a more practical combination of outdoor furniture, potted indoor plants and a wall of botanical prints.

In your hallway, any furniture style continues the sense of a garden just beyond if it is upholstered in a floral or nature-inspired fabric. Window coverings can be as simple as a sheer muslin, which allows glimpses of the outdoors while providing privacy (see page 16), or as substantial as floral-patterned draperies. Or, they can fall somewhere in the middle, such as the covering made from fringed burlap (a fabric blatantly borrowed from the garden), clipped onto rings and threaded onto copper piping, as in the entrance on page 14.

The entrance, regardless of its size, must go beyond decorative;

MIX MASTERY
A grouping of disparate elements from around the globe, drawn together by their coloring, creates a warm welcome in an entrance hall. Anchoring the collection of personal treasures is an 18th-century Italian console table with acanthus leaves carved on its cabriole legs. An exotic potted plant sits on top beside an antique horse from India, a porcelain plate and sugar bowl from England and a candlestick from a Quebec church. Beneath, vine balls top up a Greek pot and grape ivy tumbles from a bronze urn, backed by a wooden tray casually propped against the wall; above, a stylized botanical print completes the vignette.

RUSTIC CHARM

The entry (left) may be indoors, but the decorating is definitely borrowed from the garden. Simple burlap finds a new use other than protecting evergreens against harsh winter weather. A privacy provider without shutting out all sunlight, the fringed burlap hangs from a length of copper plumber's pipe. An outdoor settee plumped with cushions covered in vintage floral fabrics tucks into a corner, next to a pot of bougainvillea set on the stone tile floor. Trailing ivy hangs on the wall, which is plastered and painted to resemble rustic Italian stucco.

PERSONALITY PLUS

A sun-filled room (right) brims with hothouse charm, looking more like a greenhouse than an entrance. Reclaimed bricks on the floor, a rough-sawn wooden-frame around the doorway, architectural brackets and a concrete gargoyle found in a salvage yard all seem, at first, to be more appropriate outdoors than in. But combined with a jungle of plants, a weathered cabinet for storing gloves and scarves, and a quirky flower-decorated chandelier suspended from a ceiling stained with turquoise fabric dye, they create a welcoming space that's packed with personality and holds the promise of more to come elsewhere in the house.

it must be practical as well. Consider the lighting. Sufficient brightness is necessary for safety, but don't overlight so as to diminish a warm and welcoming mood. If the room is long and narrow, suspend a light some distance from the ceiling. If the ceiling is low, recess pot lights or mount wall sconces to provide illumination.

Providing a place to set down keys and gloves and somewhere nearby to hang coats and jackets is another welcoming, yet practical, touch. For a really small entrance, a skinny shelf mounted on delicate decorative brackets takes care of the former, while a row of pegs screwed to the wall works beautifully for the latter.

A mirror is a pleasant addition for last-minute checks before leaving the house and for guests wanting to smooth windblown

hair when they arrive. Mirrors take up no space but can add dimension to any room, particularly a small one.

Where possible — and not all entrances are large enough to accommodate this — provide a place to sit to make it easier to remove and put on shoes and boots. Small garden benches or chairs are the perfect size (see page 14).

This is the area that gets the heaviest traffic and has to keep ahead of dirty boots and dripping umbrellas. If the outside is cut stone or flagstone, the use of the same materials inside is a natural and practical continuation (see opposite). If this isn't the case, consider square black-and-white tiles set on the diagonal for a formal look, hardwood finished floors with a waterproof covering to prevent discoloration, terra-cotta tiles topped with a kilim area rug, or wall-to-wall fitted carpeting.

Since providing a welcome is the primary function of an entrance, paint it in one of the colors from the "warmer" end of the spectrum: the terra-cotta of an autumn chrysanthemum, the gold of a summer black-eyed Susan, the ivory of an autumn lily. Use space-extending paler shades of these colors and you won't be disappointed. (The colors on the "cooler" end of the spectrum — green, blue, violet and many grays — do not immediately offer a warm embrace.) Then, to tie the entrance into the balance of the house, accent it with colors or fabrics found elsewhere in other rooms.

In the end, you'll have created a room that not only welcomes you and your friends with warmth and joy, but one that sends you off with a cozy feeling. Make the last impression of the haven you call home as warm as the first. 🌿

FLAGSTONE ENTRANCE
Double doors do double duty as they open to the courtyard, as well as providing garden views all year long. The flagstone flooring continues beyond the doors to the exterior; indoors, a natural sisal carpet warms it up. Breezy curtains barely block the view of the vine-covered archway and urns of blossoming plants. Even in the winter months, a rotation of potted flowers overflow from the wicker basket, and a colorful cushion imprinted with a botanical motif softens the wicker chair.

Entrance
PROJECTS

FRAGRANT POTPOURRI

Turn a blossom-filled garden into bowls of scented petals for an all-season flower show. Set in a hallway, the potpourri will provide a scented welcome whenever the door is opened. Just choose your favorite blooms and follow these cut-and-dried steps.

SHOPPING LIST

- 4 cups dried rose petals or a mixture of other dried flowers, such as delphinium, marigolds, pansies, nemesia, lavender and yellow daisies
- 1 cup each of dried rosebuds, lavender and the dried leaves of lemon verbena, lemon balm and scented geranium
- 2 tbsp each of coarse-ground cloves, cinnamon, powdered orrisroot and grated orange or lemon rind
- 3 or 4 drops rose geranium oil

1. Select the plants that hold their color or perfume when dry. Some good bets are the flowers listed (left) and the leaves of mint, lovage, borage and raspberry.

2. Pick the flowers and leaves and spread them on a screen to dry. Set in a cool, dry, dark place. Allow a few days to a week for drying; the petals should feel like cornflakes. Store the petals separated according to color, until ready to use.

3. Mix the petals in a large bowl with your choice of herbs, spices and scented oils. Cinnamon, cardamom, nutmeg and cloves hark back to grandma's kitchen; floral oils, such as peony and lavender, stir memories of summer days (buy them from herbalists or gift shops).

4. To preserve the scents, add a fixative such as powdered orrisroot (available from herbalists).

5. Cover and set aside for two weeks to mature, stirring occasionally.

6. Set the potpourri in pretty bowls. As the fragrance diminishes with time, refresh with a drop of scented oil.

PANSY BALLS

A beautiful bowl piled high with colorful pansy balls will brighten a room or entrance area long after the garden has faded. Grow several colors in flower beds or container pots, then follow these directions on how to make perfect pansy balls.

SHOPPING LIST

- *pansy flowers*
- *nasturtium leaves (optional)*
- *silica gel*
- *Styrofoam balls, 1½ to 4 inches (4 to 10 cm) diameter*
- *white craft glue*
- *ceramic glaze*

1. Pick pansies when they are fully opened and remove the stems. Spread silica gel (a sand-like drying medium) ½ inch (1 cm) deep on the bottom of a metal or plastic pan. Lay the pansies face down in a single layer. Cover with another ½ inch (1 cm) of silica gel. Repeat with more pansies and more silica gel. Cover and set aside for about three days or until the flowers feel dry to the touch.

2. Remove the pansies and reuse the silica gel for drying other flowers. Spread a thin layer of white craft glue over about one quarter of a Styrofoam ball. Press the pansies onto the ball, overlapping the petals so none of the ball shows through.

3. Set the ball on top of a small glass to dry, then proceed with applying glue and flowers to another quarter of the ball. Set aside to dry. Continue until the ball is completely covered with pansies and dry, then paint with ceramic glaze. Let dry, then pile into a bowl or basket and use to accessorize a room.

4. For variety, dry nasturtium leaves in the same way and intersperse among the pansy flowers when covering the balls. Over time, the pansies and leaves will fade to mellow shades, especially if exposed to prolonged sunlight.

TURNING OVER A NEW LEAF

Give a plain-Jane mirror a makeover.

SHOPPING LIST

- 1 large wood-framed mirror
- fine sandpaper
- 1 (2 fl oz/59 mL) bottle green acrylic craft paint
- 1 (2 fl oz/59 mL) bottle black acrylic craft paint
- sponge
- rag cloth
- 1 (2 fl oz/59 mL) bottle acrylic craft varnish
- hot-glue gun and glue sticks
- strands of fabric ivy
- grosgrain ribbon

1. Sand the frame, then paint with a verdant green color. Let dry, then lightly sponge on black paint and wipe off immediately until only traces remain. Let dry, sand, then apply one coat of varnish.

2. Use a hot-glue gun to attach strands of fabric ivy intertwined with grosgrain ribbon.

Living Rooms

ROOMS TO RELAX IN

IN MOST HOMES, the living room is the most used, most public, space of all, so, naturally most people want it to be the most "perfect" room possible. Perfection, however, means different things to different people, but comfort, pleasure, prettiness and efficiency contribute to its creation in any room. It's how each person individually defines and then interprets each of these characteristics that results in individually "perfect" (or near-perfect!) spaces.

There is no one color to paint a living room that will guarantee a state of perfection, just as there is no one way to light it, arrange its furniture, cover its floors or embellish its windows. Some of the prettiest, most comfortable, pleasurable and most "perfect" living rooms, however, have decorating schemes inspired by the garden, a matchless source for ideas, because the garden contains pleasing color combinations, subtle lighting effects, harmonious groupings of shapes and textures and other inspirational components, which can successfully be transported to the indoors and translated into room decors.

Imagine yourself sitting in a tree-shaded garden on a hot summer's day. Sunlight filters through the overhanging branches of maple and oak trees, dappling the tabletop and the cushioned chair seats. Fragrant, colorful flowers in the surrounding beds dance in the breeze. You feel at peace. Wouldn't the same feeling be wonderful in your living room?

Start with walls painted a color you love, one you know from your garden, a color you have no doubt already included in some of your upholstered furniture or have perhaps unconsciously

ALL-SEASON CHARM
It matters not if it's winter or summer outside, this room sings with sunshine throughout the year. Plants thrive in every corner; the musical sounds of water falling from a small fountain on the right fill the room. There's even a birdhouse perched on a ledge, ready for occupancy. Bold colors for the walls, window trims and fabrics join with the verdant plants to create a personal paradise.

acquired in paintings or prints which already hang on your walls. Any color you like will make you happy as long as you remember that the warm end of the color spectrum (red, orange, yellow and their off-shoot shades, however pale) makes you feel cozy (see opposite) while the cool end of the spectrum (green, blue and violet shades, even those well diluted with white), although calming and restful, can give a room a chilly feel.

With the wall color in place, you can select floor coverings to coordinate (see below) — carpet it wall to wall, set down outdoor-inspired, hard-wearing sisal (see pages 10 and 11) or one of its cousins, such as coir, seagrass or jute — or choose to leave the floors bare, as in the room on page 26.

Contemplate the fabrics on furniture and at the windows: fabrics bursting with blooms, or patterned with faded flowers will never fail you, whether you're aiming for a formal look, a country look or a more casual feeling. If florals on the furniture or for draperies seem too much for your room, cover up with solid fabrics or small-patterned motifs and accent these unbroken

FRENCH-COUNTRY ACCENTS
A fresh coat of paint and cotton-covered cushions in bright French-country colors turn an old porch wicker settee into a new piece of living-room furniture. Chairs slipcovered to match and a wool Indo Gabbeh carpet bordered in the same shades round out the arrangement. In addition, a lively print on the wall picks up on the fabric's floral pattern.

COUNTRY CHARACTER

It's not so long ago that wicker furniture was confined to the porch or garden — but not any more. That it successfully moves indoors is apparent in a living room where a dark green wicker chair, table and planter provide a striking contrast to terra-cotta colored walls and a bold blue-checked sofa. Leafy metal-framed tables and a garden urn topped with a sheet of glass create oodles of country charm. A pottery faux fountain reminiscent of Italy decorates a wall; farmyard chickens frollc across needlepoint cushions.

(or barely broken) color blocks with floral-patterned cushions. Florals capture the essence of the garden all year long, providing a sense of contentment whatever the weather outdoors.

Lighting in a living room takes various forms depending on the type of activities that occur there and subject to your wishes to highlight some areas of the room and disguise or downplay less attractive ones. Background lighting, obtained through the use of recessed ceiling fixtures, wall lights and shade-covered table and floor lamps, is the first requirement. From there, concentrate a beam or pool of light to illuminate specific areas, such as work surfaces or reading areas, or for decorative purposes, such as calling attention to a work of art or a tabletop arrangement.

Now, what's on the walls? If paintings or prints are not yet part of the decor, this could be the time to buy some. If you wish a garden room, choosing botanical prints is a smart place to start, and they are available in all price ranges. Buy what the budget can afford and as many as possible. One large botanical print looks great; a group of four looks fabulous and makes a major statement.

As a final touch, the living room, like every room in the house, becomes more warm and welcoming if it is embellished with fresh or potted flowers and plants. They impart a sense of garden ambience and contentment. ❧

BLOOMIN' LOVELY
A background palette of pastel colors shows off garden-inspired accent pieces in a pared-down living room. Plants grow inside the wires of a pair of topiary forms, leaving the graceful curves exposed, rather than covered with trailing vines and leaves. A floral table skirt and needlepoint cushions mix with patterned ginger jars and many potted plants, baskets and vases of blossoming flowers. Belonging either indoors or out, a Corinthian column capital becomes a sturdy coffee-table base.

GARDEN-PRETTY LIVING ROOM

Floral elements blossom in profusion whatever the time of year in this sun lit living room. Floppy cushions fashioned from drapery fabric turn a sedate sofa into a comfy resting place. A variety of accents borrowed from the garden decorate the room: a wicker chair, its seat cushion covered in fabric reminiscent of an outdoor awning; oversized urns form the base for a glass-topped table; and an outdoor table holds a lamp made from a garden statue.

ANTIQUE ACCENTS

French doors in the calm, restful living room of a townhouse overlook
a trellis fence and climbing rose in the tiny back garden. Floral accents
indoors extend the sense of the garden: fabrics from the forties on the
cushions, damask covering on the sofa and the Victorian print above.
Cane-framed chairs pulled cozily up to the tapestry-covered ottoman give
the room an airy feeling; they sit on an antique floral hand-hooked rug.

PILE ON THE PATTERNS

A room this cheery creates instant happiness; its predominantly red color scheme injects a hot ambience. An abundance of flowers in myriad prints and accessories adds layers of interest and energizes everything in the room. That it is theatrical cannot be disputed: the frankly fake banana tree in the corner and oversized pansy flowers hooked into a scatter mat on the floor bring a smile to everyone who visits the room.

Living Room
PROJECTS

BLOSSOMING BULBS

Learn how to "force" bulbs — and enjoy spring flowers in your home in midwinter.

Forcing bulbs means tricking them into starting to grow earlier than they normally would. In this two-part process, you must first provide a period of cold and then a warmer temperature to encourage the flowers to develop.

Bulbs will flower about four months after you begin, so start preparations in the early fall. You can use bulbs already in your garden: the larger ones are the most reliable.

Selecting bulbs

Virtually any spring bulb can be forced: tulips, daffodils, narcissus, hyacinths, etc. The only caution is that some bulbs, such as Darwin hybrid tulips, grow over 2 feet (60 cm) tall. This may be difficult to handle in certain windowsill locations, so when you are buying bulbs, be sure to check the ultimate height of the plant.

Planting method

Use bulb pots that are a minimum of 4 inches (10 cm) deep. The diameter of the pot can be any size from 4 to 10 inches (10 to 25 cm). Be sure to plant enough bulbs per

pot. To create the best show, bulbs should be planted very close together. For example, plant 15 tulip bulbs in a 10-inch (25-cm) pot.

Use a good all-purpose potting soil and press it firmly into the bulb pot, leaving space at the top equivalent to the height of the bulb. Then push the blunt ends of the bulbs lightly into the soil. The tops of the bulbs should now be level with the lip of the pot. Add more potting soil and, lifting the pot, tap it against a table until the soil has filled all the space between the bulbs. Continue to add potting soil and repeat the tapping until the soil fills the whole pot. Follow this with a thorough watering. Use a water-soluble transplanter fertilizer (5-15-5) to promote quicker rooting.

The cool environment

Place the potted bulbs in an unheated garage in the early fall for a minimum of 12 weeks. The ideal "winter" temperature range for bulbs is from 34°F to 52°F (1°C to 9°C). Keep the soil moist during the entire cooling period.

Another method is called precooling. Before the bulbs are potted, place them in a paper bag and lightly dust them with a fungicide to prevent rotting. Then simply put them in your refrigerator and leave them there for a minimum of nine weeks — longer if you wish to stagger the flowering times. Don't put the bulbs in the freezer. This will kill them. At the end of the cooling period, pot the bulbs and place in a cool room until sprouts become visible above the soil, about three to four weeks. Keep the soil evenly moist at all times.

The warm environment

After the bulbs have received their cooling treatment, place the pots in a sunny window. Simply keep them moist (no need to fertilize) and they will bloom in as little as two weeks for crocuses to six weeks for late tulips from the time they are placed in the window.

Once in bloom, flowers will last longer if they are kept in as cool a room as possible. Failure to keep the soil moist will shorten the flowering period.

After-flowering care

When the flowers have withered, snip them, taking care not to remove any of the leaves. Keep the pots in a sunny window and let the plants continue to grow. Use a water-soluble fertilizer (15-30-15) every three weeks. When the danger of frost outside is past, plant the bulbs in the garden for flowers the following spring.

DO-IT-YOURSELF

SHOPPING LIST
- table
- wooden moldings
- mitre box and saw
- latex paint for moldings
- latex or polymer modified thin-set adhesive
- notched trowel
- tiles
- epoxy grout
- rubber-backed trowel
- sponge
- acrylic sealer
- stencils
- ceramic stencil paints
- stencil brushes
- nails

FIT TO BE TILED

Turn a tired wooden table into a stunning showpiece.

1. Clean the tabletop. Lay out the tiles to determine their placement. Cut moldings to fit around the perimeter. Mitre the corners if you wish. Paint the moldings with at least two coats of latex paint. Set aside.

2. Mix the adhesive and spread on the table following the manufacturer's instructions. Use a notched trowel to form swirling ridges.

4. Mix the grout according to the manufacturer's directions. Using a rubber-backed trowel, force the grout firmly into the spaces between the tiles. Use a damp sponge to wipe off excess grout. Let the grout dry.

3. Press the tiles firmly onto the adhesive, leaving a ⅛-inch (3-mm) space between them. Let set overnight. (If desired, cover the tiles with a large piece of wood and hammer with a rubber mallet to be certain the tiles are well affixed.)

5. Apply acrylic sealer to the tiles and let dry. Stencil the design onto the tiles and let dry, then seal with two more coats of acrylic sealer.

6. Nail on the moldings. Countersink the nails, fill with grout or wood filler; let dry and paint the filler.

SHEER GENIUS

Cotton muslin or other sheer fabric delivers pared-down style, provides glimpses of the garden and blows gently in the breeze of an open window.

SHOPPING LIST

- *enough fabric for 1½ times the window width, plus the appropriate length so it will cascade onto the floor*
- *matching thread*
- *gold cord*
- *brass rings*
- *brass rod and brackets*

1. Machine stitch the panels together to give the desired width.

2. Press under all the top, bottom and side edges ¼ inch (5 mm), twice. Pin in place, then machine stitch.

3. Hand stitch gold cord along the top edge. Stitch brass rings along the top edge, about 12 inches (30 cm) apart. Thread onto a brass rod and mount on the brackets.

DO-IT-YOURSELF

MATERIAL GAINS

Old drapery fabrics put fresh floral faces on cushions styled for today's interiors.

SHOPPING LIST
- *drapery fabrics from the thirties and forties*
- *thread*
- *cushion forms*
- *decorative trims (optional)*

1. Dry-clean old draperies before using. Check that no holes or tears exist in the fabric to be used. Measure a cushion form. Cut two pieces of fabric from an attractive section of the old drapes, adding an extra 1½ inches (4 cm) to the measured size of the form.

2. Machine or hand stitch the trim in place as desired on one or both pieces. Pin the two pieces right sides together and machine stitch around three sides, ¾ inch (2 cm) in from the edges. Turn right-side out and press. Stuff the cushion form into the casing. Pin the opening closed, tucking in the raw edges ¾ inch (2 cm). Slip stitch together using matching thread.

3. For a fancier, more flouncy cushion, rim it with a ruffle made from the fabric. Cut a piece of fabric 8 inches (20 cm) wide and the length of the perimeter of the cushion, plus an additional 6 inches (15 cm). (If necessary, cut several pieces of fabric and join them together to obtain the correct size.) Machine sew the two short ends together, right-sides together. Press the seam open, then turn right side out. Fold the fabric in half lengthwise, right-side out, and press the long raw edges together. Using a very long stitch, machine sew the two long edges together.

4. Lay the raw edge of the ruffle piece along a raw edge of right side of the front cover piece. Pin a section in place. About 2 inches (5 cm) from the corner, pull on the under thread of the ruffle and gather into a flounce. Pin in place, gathering the flounce about 2 inches (5 cm) around the corner. Then pin a straight section together along an edge and gather again about 2 inches (5 cm) from each corner. Baste in place.

5. Lay the back cover piece right-side down on top of the front and ruffle piece. Machine sew together as for a plain cushion. Stuff with the cushion form and hand sew closed.

GOOD CHEMISTRY

Groups of bottles usually found in a science lab make innovative flower holders.

SHOPPING LIST

• *3 or more science-lab bottles (available from laboratory equipment suppliers)*
• *flowers with sparse florets on long, thin stems, such as anenomes, ranunculas, orchids, freesia, iris and/or thin grasses available from florists*

1. Fill the bottles with about 2 inches (5 cm) of lukewarm water.

2. Set one or two stems of flowers and grass in each bottle. Group three together on a table or set several in a long row along a mantel or windowsill.

GILDED SHADE

Get a glow on a lampshade with a floral stamp.

SHOPPING LIST

- *peel-and-stick lampshade*
- *plain cotton fabric*
- *1 (2 oz/59 mL) bottle gold acrylic textile paint, or 1 (2 oz/59 mL) bottle gold acrylic craft paint and 1 (2 oz/59 mL) bottle textile medium*
- *small foam roller*
- *rubber stamp*
- *iron*
- *fringe or trim*
- *white craft glue*

1. Remove the paper wrapping from a peel-and-stick lampshade and use it as a pattern to cut out the fabric.

2. Pour acrylic textile paint onto a plate. (Or, if using regular acrylic craft paint, mix it with textile medium following manufacturer's instructions.) Roll the foam roller through the paint, then pass the roller across the design of the rubber stamp. Test the stamp on spare fabric. Adjust the amount of paint on the rubber stamp and press on the fabric where desired.

3. Let dry, then iron following the manufacturer's instructions to set the paint.

4. Attach the fabric to the sticky surface of the shade. Turn under the raw edge and glue it in place. Attach fringe or trim to the top and bottom rims with craft glue.

SNAPPY SCRAP CUSHIONS

It's the details that make the difference. Sew cushion covers following the general directions on page 36. Look at the designer-type options in this cache of cushions and create them yourself.

SHOPPING LIST
- *scraps of floral fabrics*
- *thread*
- *fringe, trim, cord*
- *cushion form*

1. Sew a patchwork-type cover by first sewing nine squares of silk fabric into a central front panel. Add a contrasting border around the squared centre, covering the seam with machine-stitched trim. Pin the fringe between the back and front panels before sewing them together, as directions indicate for the flounced border on one of the vintage cushions on page 36.

2. The pillow in front has a central panel like the patchwork one, and grosgrain ribbon in place of the fringe. The same ribbon forms jaunty bows sewn at the corners for a perky effect.

3. The pillow in back is a combination of the two and is trimmed with multicolored cord, hand sewn to the cushion after it has been stuffed with its form.

BLIND AMBITION

An easy stencil treatment gives a decorator look to an inexpensive window blind.

SHOPPING LIST
- *roller blind, sized to fit*
- *stencil that matches room decor*
- *oil-based stencil paints*
- *stencil adhesive spray or masking tape*
- *stencil brushes*
- *mineral spirits*
- *tassel and trim (optional)*
- *hot-glue gun and glue sticks (optional)*

1. Spray the underside of the stencil with adhesive to make it stick to the surface of the blind or use masking tape to hold it in place. Dab a stencil brush in paint, then dab onto the blind, using as little paint as possible. Be sure to use a small stencil brush for small openings, a larger brush for larger openings. Reposition the stencils to create the desired pattern. Set aside until dry; the time varies depending on the type of paint used. Clean brushes with mineral spirits.

2. Use a glue gun to decorate the bottom of the blind with trim and a pull tassel if desired.

HANG UPS

Make a stunning wall decoration with a pair of reverse-découpage plates suspended from a ribbon.

SHOPPING LIST

- *pretty images cut from cards, books or magazines*
- *2 clear plates, 8 inches (20 cm) in diameter*
- *découpage scissors*
- *white craft glue*
- *gold metallic marker*
- *frosted silver spray paint*
- *5-inch (12.5-cm) wide ribbon*
- *2 plate hangers*
- *1 plastic or metal ring, ½ inch (1 cm) in diameter*
- *3 nails*

1. Cut pretty images from cards, books or magazines.

2. Clean and dry 2 clear plates. Spread clear-drying white craft glue to the fronts of the images. Then attach face down to the underside of the plates.

3. When the glue has dried, outline selected images with a gold pen on the underside to add glitter and highlights.

4. Spray the back with frosted paint to fill in spaces between the paper images.

5. Attach the plate hangers to the decorated plates. Make a bow as illustrated. Sew a ½-inch (1-cm) diameter ring to the back of the bow and use to hang on a nail on the wall. Drive 2 more nails through the ribbon into the wall for hanging the plates.

ARMCHAIR FARMING

Planting a crop in decorative containers produces almost-instant greenery.

SHOPPING LIST
• *decorative bowls, pots or other watertight containers*
• *small stones*
• *potting soil*
• *wheat, flax or alfalfa seeds (available at health-food stores)*

1. Place a layer of small stones in the bottom of a container. (If using an old wooden crate or box, line it with a plastic food container or other watertight container.) Top with a 2- to 3-inch (5- to 8-cm) layer of potting soil. Barely moisten the soil.

2. Scatter a thin layer of seeds over the surface, then top with another thin layer of soil. Moisten sparingly. Set indoors in a warm sunny spot and watch the crops grow! Water daily or as necessary to keep the soil barely moist. Wheat will grow to 7 inches (18 cm) in height in a week, flax to 4 inches (10 cm) and alfalfa to about 2 inches (5 cm). Beyond that height, the plants tend to fall over and become unattractive, so simply repeat the process for another crop. This is an excellent way to obtain a broad decorative "surface" of greenery for a short time.

Dining Rooms & Kitchens
FEASTS FOR THE EYES

No OTHER ROOMS in the house lend themselves so well to garden-inspired decorating as the dining room and kitchen, especially since today's style of day-to-day living and special entertaining tends to be far more casual than in years gone by.

In many homes, the "formal" dining room has been down-sized or perhaps even eliminated altogether in favor of a new approach: an expanded kitchen which also accommodates an eating area. This not only allows for family and guests to be part of meal preparation, it permits the cook to be part of the fun!

Universally considered the heart of a home, the kitchen — and its eating component, whatever form it takes — invites friends and family to remain long after the meal is finished. Wherever the food is prepared and the dining takes place, however, inspiration for the decoration of these rooms flourishes just outside in the garden.

Dining rooms and kitchens, like all other rooms, get stamped

MEDITERRANEAN MAGIC

Whatever the season, an Italian-villa-inspired dining room feels warm and inviting. Sheer curtains fringed and swagged soften large windows, which overlook a lake. A mixture of furniture styles keeps the room casual: a worn and rustic trestle table, surrounded by Shaker-style chairs interpreted in up-to-the-minute brushed aluminum; a fashionable fifties metal-legged chair; an Italian-inspired marble and wrought-iron console table on which rests a terra-cotta medallion; standard candlesticks from an old church; and covering much of the floor, a rough sisal carpet. Even though the trees outside are without their leaves, there's a sense of sheltered courtyard calm in the dining room.

HARVEST SUPPER

A fireside dinner setting reflects the season with table decorations made from harvest produce. Bouquets of wheat tied with black satin bows brighten the backs of the antique chairs. Miniature wheat sheaves stand sentry on the mantel; sprays of seed heads surround the candle bases of the black-shaded chandelier. A pottery café-au-lait cup holds a bouquet of fresh flowers. Dishes and cutlery take their color cues from the flowers in the quilt, which is used as a table covering.

with a certain personality . . . they may be warm and cozy, light and elegant or perhaps reminiscent of a conservatory.

In the first type of kitchen/dining room, rich bold colors on the walls, wooden shutters at the windows, a dark carpet on the floor and accents of brass will create the "look." On the walls, paintings with garden-fresh floral or food themes appropriately set the mood for cozy dining. A low slung chandelier focused directly on the table will provide dramatic lighting. In the kitchen, cabinets and flooring may be wood that has been stained a deep color. Lighting strips mounted on the underside of overhead cabinets provide direct illumination on countertops and other food-preparation surfaces, without filling the room with harsh overall lighting.

Light and elegant nature-inspired dining rooms and kitchens get their feeling from pastel pink-, yellow- or green-colored walls, soft floral or sheer fabrics at the windows, glass-top tables, pale wood, light-colored floor coverings and glass accents such as candlesticks and accessories. White cabinets or those given a pale painted wash treatment, some with glazed doors that reveal their pretty contents, and white back-splash tiles brighten a kitchen. A plate rack stacked with floral china or wall-mounted floral plates, such as those featured in the kitchen on page 49, diverts the eye to details.

GOING FOR BAROQUE
The burnished colors and elaborate ornamentation of a buffet tableau recall a 17th-century baroque setting, but it is constructed from thoroughly modern materials, including the ornately carved reproduction table and dramatically framed still life with flowers propped up against the wall. Fresh ivy spills out of a champagne bucket and trails around glass stems and forest-green napkins, which are sponge-painted with gold leaf motifs and folded to hold cutlery. Fresh pears fill the bottom tier of an antique epergne and surround chunky candles that flank the table.

The conservatory-like kitchen/dining room comes together by combining cane or bamboo furniture, a glass-topped table, metal and wood-slatted chairs, jungle-printed or bold floral fabrics and terra-cotta tile flooring. For variety in texture, a sisal carpet under the dining table makes a practical choice (see page 42).

These rooms lend themselves to whimsical decorative accents, which add an element of surprise and make them memorable, such as a vase of brightly colored paper flowers bought in Mexico, a bowl of looks-good-enough-to-eat papier-mâché vegetables, a basket of shiny ceramic fruits, a collection of miniature geese and ducks.

Wherever the actual dining takes place, head to the garden for something to brighten the centre of the table. Every season produces its unique bounty ready for the plucking. In the spring, early-blooming snowdrops, scillas and primulas gathered together in small glass or silver-colored containers and set at each place setting create a fresh look after a long winter. Later, a basket lined with a waterproof container becomes the perfect hold-all for an armload of garden-picked roses or a colorful combination of delphiniums, snapdragons, cosmos and daisies.

Assorted autumnal vegetables, piled in a pyramid on a base of colorful maple leaves and intertwined with sinuous vines, appropriately celebrate the harvest season. Later, strands of English ivy, brightly berried holly and plush clusters of pine needles stretching the length of the table in a casual garland announce December festivities with flair.

Even small garden touches can create a big effect: for instance, bunches of dried flowers never lose their appeal and can brighten a kitchen all year long as the room on this page shows. Tendrils of ivy twisted around napkins (which themselves have been stamped with a gold leaf image) make imaginative napkin rings. Even a single rose in an antique bottle can change a ho-hum table into a stylish setting. 🦊

CUT AND DRIED

Dried flowers suggest summer in a wintertime kitchen. Modest bouquets of various blossoms, such as yarrow, strawflower, statice and globe amaranth, gain impact when tied together in bunches and attached to the metal hood of an exhaust fan suspended above a counter-mounted cook-top. More burst out of a brass container mounted on the wall. And above the country-kitchen dining table, tendrils of vibrant bittersweet cling to the branches of the iron-and-wood electric chandelier.

OPEN-ENDED KITCHEN

A galley kitchen that links an entrance hall to a dining room takes advantage of the two areas it connects. One end opens onto a tall window with garden views, in front of which sits a Victorian wire garden settee softened with floral-patterned cushions. The opposite end opens onto the garden-inspired dining room (see pages 10 and 11). The same fabric that covers the chair seats hides cleaning supplies beneath the kitchen sink.

GARDEN KITCHEN

Ceiling-high windows and the sliding-glass door in the sunny kitchen of a suburban home suggest being in the middle of the garden all year round. Italian pottery decorated with flowers and floral-patterned back-splash tiles add to that summer feeling. The white metal chair pulled up to the desk is reminiscent of outdoor garden furniture; set on Mexican tile flooring, it suits the casual style of the kitchen.

Dining Room & Kitchen
PROJECTS

BASKET CASE

A simple wooden basket filled with flowers converts to a casual centrepiece for a dining-room table.

1. Clean and dry a wooden fruit basket and line the bottom with aluminum foil.

2. Insert 3 or 4 pots of blooming flowers, such as geraniums, primulas, chrysanthemums, pansies and cineraria.

3. Tuck Spanish moss between the leaves and the basket edge.

SHOPPING LIST
- *wooden fruit basket*
- *aluminum foil*
- *3 or 4 pots of blooming flowers*
- *Spanish moss*

HERB APPEAL

Perk up windowsills all year long with these attractive and unusual herb planters.

1. Put a 1-inch (2.5-cm) deep layer of small stones in the bottom of each can. Top with potting soil.

2. Plant herbs and set on a sunny kitchen windowsill. Water sparingly. Snip herbs as desired to add fresh flavor to cooking.

SHOPPING LIST
- *empty cans with colorful labels*
- *small stones*
- *potting soil*
- *herbs, such as parsley, oregano, rosemary, chives and basil*

FENCED IN

Corral your favorite herbs or flowers in a fenced-in planter

SHOPPING LIST
- *mini-picket-fence sections, approximately 5 or 6 inches (12.5 or 15 cm) high*
- *⅝-inch (1.5-cm) plywood*
- *½-inch (1-cm) paintbrush*
- *white semigloss latex paint*
- *carpenter's glue*
- *sandpaper*
- *decorative ribbon*
- *potted herbs (or flowers)*

1. Buy mini-picket fencing at craft stores. (This one uses two 8-picket sections for each long side and one 6-picket section for each short end.)

2. For the bottom of the planter, cut a piece of plywood the correct size to fit inside the pickets when they are placed erect. Paint all sides of the bottom board and pickets with several coats of paint, sanding between coats.

3. Glue the picket sections along the edges of the bottom board. Glue the picket uprights together at the corners.

4. Let dry, then tie with a jaunty ribbon and bow. Fill with small pots of herbs set in small saucers. Water sparingly. Change the ribbon and bow for a different look.

DO-IT-YOURSELF

SWITCHED ON

Lighten a room with garden-gorgeous switch plates.

SHOPPING LIST

- *switch-plate cover(s)*
- *fine sandpaper*
- *floral wallpaper or fabric, or photocopies of seed packets*
- *scissors*
- *craft knife*
- *tacky glue*
- *acrylic craft varnish*
- *acrylic craft paint and small artist's brush*
- *awl*

1. Remove plastic switch-plate covers from a wall or buy new ones. Clean thoroughly, then sand lightly with fine sandpaper.

2. Prepare the covering, using wallpaper, fabric or photocopies. Place the covering wrong-side up on a flat surface and trace an outline of the switch plate. Make sure the image appears centred and properly framed on the front. Trace around the centre hole. Cut out the covering, allowing a ½-inch (1-cm) margin all around. Use a craft knife to score an X from corner to corner inside the switch hole, thus creating four triangular-shaped flaps.

3. Cut the four outside corners diagonally to remove a bit of the covering.

4. Spread tacky glue over the underside of the paper or fabric. Position on front of the switch plate. Press firmly in place, easing out air bubbles. Turn the outside edges and little flaps in the centre to the underside and press in place. Let dry.

5. Apply at least three coats of acrylic varnish, drying between coats. Paint screws to match the pattern if you wish. Use an awl to poke holes in the switch plate for screws. Remount on the wall.

LIGHTEN UP
*Use this pattern to make
your own candle shades.*

1. Enlarge this page by 20 percent
on a photocopier.

2. Cut out the candle-shade
pattern superimposed on the
photograph. Trace onto heavyweight iron-on
interfacing and then onto the fabric. Cut out
the shapes. Cut off the flap (dotted-line
portion) on the interfacing.

3. Following the manufacturer's instructions,
iron interfacing onto the underside of the
fabric.

4. Spread a thin line of craft glue on
the underside of the flap.
Fold inside and press against
the interfacing. Let dry,
then apply a thin line of glue
to the folded flap; bend and press
onto the unglued edge to create the
shade and hold until dry.

5. Glue trim to the top and bottom edges
for a decorative finish.

6. Mount on a candle follower. Use dripless
candles only. Never leave lit candles unattended.

SHOPPING LIST
(for individual shade)
- *12 inches (0.3 m) cotton fabric*
- *12 inches (0.3 m) heavyweight
  iron-on interfacing*
- *white craft glue*
- *32 inches (0.8 m) trim*
- *candle follower (a metal
  support for the shade)*

SERVIETTES WITH STYLE

Stamp your personality on these handmade napkins.

SHOPPING LIST
- *lightweight cotton muslin or ready-made cotton napkins*
- *sharp knife*
- *miniature artichokes, sugar pears, tiny apples and star fruit*
- *fabric paint or acrylic craft paint mixed with textile medium according to manufacturer's instructions*

1. Prewash lightweight cotton muslin and cut into 15-inch (38-cm) squares. Iron the edges to the wrong side in a double fold and machine stitch in place. If using ready-made napkins, wash and press.

2. Using a sharp knife, cut miniature artichokes, sugar pears, tiny apples or star fruit in half.

3. Pour a small amount of fabric paint into a saucer and thin with a little water. Press cut side of fruits in the paint, dab off on a piece of newspaper, then press onto the napkins.

4. Let dry, then press with a hot iron according to directions on the paint to set it.

ON THE FLOOR FRONT

Instead of a carpet on a wood floor, why not stencil a rug? If the floor is varnished, have the varnish professionally removed and the floor sanded.

SHOPPING LIST
- *roller and paint tray*
- *white latex floor paint*
- *1-inch (2.5-cm) paintbrush*
- *stencils*
- *masking tape*
- *latex stencil paints in several shades*
- *stencil brushes, one for each color*
- *roller refill or brush to apply varnish*
- *latex varnish*

1. Paint or roll on two coats of white latex floor paint, using a brush in the corners and along edges. Use a pencil to outline the rug and mark its centre.

2. Use several stencils and several shades of paint to create your rug, fixing the stencils in place with masking tape.

3. Use as little paint on the brushes as possible. For a firm finish, paint or roll on two coats of latex varnish after the paints have dried. Not recommended for high traffic areas.

LEMON AID

Simple table decorations take their fruity cue from the pattern on the chinaware.

SHOPPING LIST

- *2 to 3 dozen unblemished lemons*
- *6 branches salal leaves (available at florists)*
- *1 sheet mylar (available at artists' supply stores)*
- *marker pen*

FOR THE CENTREPIECE: Line a plate about 14 inches (35 cm) in diameter with salal leaves. Form a base layer of lemons, all the ends points out. Continue to add more layers of lemons in the same way, forming a pyramid shape. Tuck salal leaves among the lemons.

FOR THE CANDLE HOLDERS: Use a sharp knife or grapefruit knife to form a hole in each lemon top, sized to hold a candle upright. If necessary, shape the lemon bottoms to fit onto the candlesticks. Tuck salal leaves around the bases of the candles where they fit into the lemons. Do not leave lit candles unattended.

FOR THE PLACE-NAME HOLDERS: Cut a 1-inch (2.5-cm) slit in a lemon. Cut out pieces of mylar about 2 inches (5 cm) high and 3 inches (8 cm) long. Use a marker pen to write guests' names in the centre. Tuck mylar into the slit in the lemon and set one at each place setting.

TABLE DRESSING

Quilted placemats dress a dining table in style.

SHOPPING LIST

- *several floral cotton fabrics*
- *thread*
- *fabric for undersides of placemats*
- *thin polyester quilt batting or flannelette*
- *bias seam binding (optional)*

1. Cut strips of floral fabric in several widths. With the right sides together, sew the strips into 14x17-inch (35x43-cm) pieces. Cut a piece of fabric for the underside of each placemat the same size as the pieced-together top. Cut a piece of quilt batting or flannelette the same size to put between the two layers.

2. Lay the backing piece wrong-side up on a flat surface. Top with the middle layer of quilt batting (or flannelette). Lay the stitched-together piece, right-side up, on top of that. Pin the three layers together or baste in place.

3. Using a fine needle, sew rows of small stitches through all three layers following the seam lines, thus quilting the pieces together.

4. Using purchased bias seam binding (or make your own by cutting 1½-inch [4-cm] wide strips of placemat fabric on the diagonal), sew the three layers together around the edges.

KEEPING TABS

Easy-to-sew tab tops pretty up all window shapes.

SHOPPING LIST

• enough fabric for 1½ times the window width and appropriate length plus hems at the top and bottom and an additional ¼ to ½ yard (22 to 45 cm) for tabs
• matching thread
• rod and brackets

1. First, make the tabs: Cut fabric strips 5 inches (12.5 cm) wide. Fold in half lengthwise, right sides together, and sew along the long raw edges. Turn right-side out, place the seam down the centre and press flat. Cut into 8-inch (20-cm)-long pieces to make tabs. (The number of tabs depends on the width of the window; they should be spaced about 4 inches (10 cm) apart.)

2. Cut a 4-inch (10-cm) wide strip of fabric the width of the curtains to use as a facing. Sew a ¼-inch (5-mm) double hem along one long raw edge. Fold the tabs in half, raw ends together, seam inside. Pin to the right side of the curtain fabric along the top edge, about 4 inches (10 cm) apart, raw edges aligned. Pin the facing strip to the curtain, right sides together. Machine stitch along the top edge and two side edges, ¾ inch (2 cm) from the edges. Flip the facing to the back and press. Hem the sides and bottoms of the curtains.

3. Thread the tabs onto a decorative rod and mount.

Bedrooms & Bathrooms
PERSONAL SPACES, PRIVATE RETREATS

SET APART FROM the shared spaces and public areas of a house, bedrooms and bathrooms lend themselves to being intimately personalized. The only rooms you can really call your own, they offer an opportunity for the purest expression of your unique and individual style. They are also, by nature of their privacy, the perfect places to indulge in favorite colors and fanciful decorating. Retreats and refuges from the details of the day, they're where you go for restorative relaxation and rejuvenation.

To soothe and refresh the spirit, bedrooms and baths should be as peaceful and quiet as a forest glade, as calm as a walled garden at nightfall. Color becomes one of the most important considerations in creating a restful, comforting space: very pale pinks, blues, greens and turquoise are particularly tranquil shades, along with pure or creamy whites as in the bedroom on page 63.

Some people, however, prefer to be refreshed and stimulated not by serene shades but by colors and patterns, so they'll opt for livelier, bolder statements, as the owners of the bedroom on this page do. For them, motifs from nature interpreted in fabrics and accessories provide the rejuvenation they seek.

BLOSSOMING BED-SIT
With no access to a garden, high-rise residents retreat to their bedroom when they feel the need for an outdoor experience. Jaunty auriculas punctuate the grassy-green fabric used on the bedspread and sofa; louvred shutters filter the light and conceal the lack of a garden beyond. Potted plants, a jug of flowers and a ficus benjamina (uplit to throw spidery shadows on the walls and ceiling at night) create a pretend garden up on the eighteenth floor.

AGE OF INNOCENCE

Bucolic pastoral scenes depicted in pale pink *toile de Jouy* fabric and paper cover the bed linens and walls of a romantically feminine bedroom. Pencil pleats gather the fabric into a modest corona above the antique iron-and-brass bed. The same fabric covers the fringed bedside lamps.

PAINTED PANELS

The raised-panel doors and built-in drawers of an attic bedroom get star status with hand-painted flower and leaf motifs. A stencil treatment would work equally well. For the small child who's too big for a crib, a miniature pine bed is the perfect place to sleep. A short dowel, threaded with buttercup-yellow chintz fabric, then mounted to the wall, turns into a canopy that frames the bed.

But it takes more than just color and pattern to create a haven. The bed is the primary comfort component in this most personal of rooms, its size and style at the discretion of its occupant or occupants. A comfy mattress and a supportive headboard are the most important elements of the bed; decorating it is the fun part, and it is something that can be quickly changed with the seasons or a shift in mood. Often flowers and other garden scenes inspire the decorative patterns on bedcoverings and surrounding walls, as the delightful room on page 60 shows.

Tables and lights on either side of the bed are essential and should suit the needs of the sleepers. While soft lighting can illuminate the whole room, directional side lights mean you or your partner can read without disturbing the other.

Underfoot, a carpeted floor pampers the early riser and makes pottering about your private room a warm and cozy activity. A small television, a comfy chair with a lamp beside it and a table for flowers, books, reading glasses and a teacup put everything within reach before you head to bed.

Providing appropriate window coverings is a challenge in decorating a bedroom. Some sleepers, who are unaffected by outside light and have no privacy concerns, can hang floaty voile curtains, which stir softly in a summer night's breeze. Others require heavy, lined draperies to shut out all sense of life beyond the window (and possible prying eyes); these create a delicious cosseting ambience on a stormy winter's night.

Very different needs such as these can both be satisfied through the use of shutters as window treatments. Often thought of as imaginative outdoor embellishments to a house, they make a fashionable decorating statement indoors as well. The owners of the bedroom opposite fling open the shutters — and the windows — in summer. Those who live in the bedroom on page 58 curl up on their floral-patterned sofa or under their matching bedspread with all the louvres tightly closed when the summer sun rises at five in the morning or winter snow blows against their high-rise condominium walls.

ATTIC AERIE
Garden-green shutters close across a dormer window, creating a cozy under-the-eaves bedroom in an older home. Dramatic black-and-white *toile de Jouy* fabric covers an old loveseat; matching cushions cozy it up. A contemporary take on a four-poster bed provides a sense of antiquity without crowding the small room.

Shutters make excellent window coverings in a bathroom as well, their louvres opened slightly for air movement while maintaining desired privacy. And like the bedroom, an exclusive bathroom is a personal sanctuary, where you can pamper yourself amid a cozy personalized decor.

While bathrooms need to satisfy both those in a hurry to get ready for work and those who want to sit back and soak at the end of the day, their decor need not suffer. A shower separate from the tub is a desirable luxury, easily achieved through careful space planning. Surrounding the tub with fragrant flowers or luxurious plants and potions for soothing the body creates a spa-in-the-home for immediate indulgences.

A treetop view through nearby windows (sees page 66 and 67) or overhead skylights that reveal fluffy clouds in a blue sky (see opposite) add to the sense of peace and well-being that a long, luxurious bath guarantees.

Creative lighting, from several sources, contributes to a well functioning bath. Lighting above the shower and over the vanity or sinks aid activities in those areas. Overall illumination is a must: a fanciful chandelier or wall-mounted sconces are options; a dimmer switch allows for either bright lights or a subdued mood during soothing nighttime bathing.

Sinks can be set in vanity counters, stand proud on pedestals or be inset in antique dressers adapted to take them. The mirrors above can be fancifully framed to match the look.

Walls might be painted or papered in calming colors that relate to the bedroom; decorative motifs borrowed from nature, such as the trellis in the small bathroom opposite and the trellis-patterned wallpaper on page 68, suggest the refreshing ambience of a summer garden. Touches such as these turn an ordinary bath into a sybaritic retreat. 🥀

A ROOM WITH NO VIEW
An overhead skylight welcomes sunshine into an interior bathroom. With no views to overlook, an outdoor trellis mounted on one wall inspires thoughts of a wished-for garden. Ivy trailing over the mirror appears eager to attach itself to the trellis to create a verdant wall covering in the near future.

SITTING PRETTY

With walls painted to resemble aged Italian stucco and antique French-silk curtains woven in a delicate floral pattern, a sybaritic bathroom invites the simple pleasure of a leisurely soak in its arresting focal point: a deep 19th-century footed tub. Gothic-style windows reclaimed from a demolished church frame views of the garden outside. Sunshine filtered through the trees bathes the room with a soft light. Wall-to-wall sisal carpeting adds a rough organic note to an otherwise pretty and pastel room.

BOLD AND BEAUTIFUL

The assertive pattern of a floral fabric lends itself to reinterpretation in other ways as this bathroom shows. Sparingly used at the tall narrow window and attached with Velcro™ to the antiquated sink, the fabric also decorates the molding strip joining the wainscotted paneling to the wall.

MINI-GARDEN ACCENTS

Decorative details give a city bathroom a country mood: gathered lace at the window, paneled cabinetry and a tiled countertop. Garden accents embellish the room, set against a background of wallpaper printed with a rose-colored trellis pattern. A dried-flower topiary on the counter and a floral needlepoint rug on the hardwood floor play up the garden theme.

Bedroom & Bathroom
PROJECTS

LATTICE LEAF

Build a lattice headboard in under an hour.

SHOPPING LIST

- *one 4x8-foot sheet white PVC lattice*
- *two 8-foot strips white channeled PVC molding trim*
- *straight saw*
- *mitre box*
- *wire or screws*

---

1. Decide on the width and the height of the headboard, depending on the size of the bed. Use a straight saw to cut the lattice to size.

2. Measure the length of the molding trim to fit the two side edges and along the top edge of the headboard.

3. Use a mitre box to cut 45-degree angles at both ends of the top strip and one end of each side strip.

4. Slip the lattice into the channels. Wire the bottom edge of the headboard to the bed frame or screw to the wall. (PVC lattice is available at most hardware stores.)

PICKET LINE

Brighten a child's room with an easy-to-make picket-fence headboard.

SHOPPING LIST

• *nine 4-foot-long pine pickets*
• *one 8-foot length 1 x 2-inch pine, cut into two pieces, each the desired width of the headboard*
• *36 1¼-inch screws*
• *1 quart (1 L) white semigloss latex paint*
• *2-inch (5-cm) paintbrush*
• *sandpaper*

1. To make a headboard suitable for a single bed, lay 9 pickets on the floor, spacing them about 1 inch (2.5 cm) apart and in the desired pattern.

2. Screw crosspieces cut to fit to the pickets on the back, about 1 foot (30 cm) from the top and bottom edges.

3. Paint with three coats of paint, sanding between coats. Screw to the wall.

BLOOMIN' BEAUTIFUL

Pretty up a cushion with a floral print.

SHOPPING LIST

- *white or ivory cotton fabric or light-color cushion cover*
- *waxed paper*
- *color photocopy of a floral print*
- *transfer medium*
- *paper towel*
- *rolling pin*
- *1-inch (2.5-cm) paintbrush*
- *small flat sponge*
- *colored cotton fabric and sewing machine, if making own cushion*

1. Lay the fabric on a flat surface with a piece of waxed paper beneath, or, if using an existing cushion cover, place a piece of cardboard covered with waxed paper inside.

2. Cut the photocopied image to the desired size, then lay image-side up on another piece of waxed paper to protect your tabletop.

3. Brush a thin layer of transfer medium over the image. Turn the image upside down onto the fabric. Cover with a piece of paper towel. Press firmly in place with a rolling pin. Remove the paper towel. If any medium has seeped out at the edges, wipe away with a damp sponge. Let dry overnight. Moisten the photocopied image with a wet sponge. Leave for 30 seconds, then drag a sponge across the paper to peel it off. The image will remain on the fabric. Repeat sponging several times until the image is perfectly clear. Sew into a cushion as shown, or if using an existing cushion cover, stuff with a cushion form.

Tray Chic

*Breakfast in bed is more relaxing when it's
served on a fancy fabric-covered tray.*

Shopping List
- *1 craft-store wooden tray*
- *sandpaper*
- *latex semigloss paint*
- *cotton fabric*
- *white craft glue*
- *acrylic varnish*
- *craft knife*

1. Sand the wooden tray and paint with several coats of latex semigloss paint, sanding between each dried coat.

2. Lay the tray flat on the wrong side of the cotton fabric. (A traditional toile fabric is nice because it is printed with a pretty pastoral scene, but any floral pattern works well.) Roughly measure the height of the side and end pieces, mark this on the fabric, then cut out.

3. Lay the fabric inside the tray with the wrong-side up. Use a pencil to mark exactly the size required. Remove from the tray. Cut squares out at each corner, leaving a ¼-inch (0.5-cm) seam allowance, and mitre into the corners exactly where the fabric will sit in the tray.

4. Press the seam allowances to the underside on the end pieces of the fabric. Spread white craft glue over the bottom of the tray and press the fabric in place, right-side up. Spread glue on the sides, press the fabric in place, curving the seam allowance onto ends. Glue the end pieces in place.

5. Let dry, then varnish with several coats of acrylic varnish. Use a craft knife to trim off any excess fabric along the top edges and to cut holes if tray has handles.

A Stitch in Time

*Delicate embroideries that you've collected or inherited come
to life in frames.*

Embroideries, laces and tatting are fun to collect. They make beautiful wall decorations when they are professionally mounted and framed. If the textiles are in good condition, a qualified framer can easily mount them on color-accenting acid-free paper and enclose them in glass and a frame.

If a little touch-up work is required before framing, the services of a textile restorer or art mender should be sought. Ask at art galleries or museums for recommended tradespeople.

Several pieces of textiles, mounted in the same frames, look beautiful when grouped together on a wall.

Do-It-Yourself

FOOLED YOU!

A trompe l'oeil scene painted on a basement bedroom wall makes you think you can walk straight out into the garden.

It would take an artistic person to re-create a scene like this on any wall, but hope waits in wallpaper books for those less talented! Many companies such as Decorlex and Komar manufacture wallpaper panels depicting pastoral and garden scenes.

For the best look, apply a wallpaper panel to the wall, following the manufacturer's directions, then nail on molding strips to create a doorway which frames the vista. Mount a drapery rod above and hang curtains or drapery panels from it. Alternately, affix a smaller wallpaper panel to the wall, cut to fit inside a new or antique window frame. After the wallpaper has dried, nail or screw the window frame to the wall.

NO-SEW BILLOWY CURTAINS

For a small dormer window, hang sheer curtains, handkerchief style. They'll blow in the breeze and show off the outdoors.

SHOPPING LIST

- *thin polyester sheer curtain fabric 1½ times the width of the window and the length from hanging point at the top to the windowsill plus about 15 inches (38 cm) for fold over*
- *scissors*
- *drapery ring clips*
- *2 eye screws, ½ inch (1 cm) in diameter*
- *aircraft cable and 2 turn buckles (available at hardware stores)*
- *brass plumb bob (optional)*

1. Determine where to mount the wire to hold the curtains and measure the distance from there to the windowsill. Fold over the fabric, forming a cuff about 15 inches (38 cm) deep. Press lightly in place. Cut the cuff into deep handkerchief points about 15 inches (38 cm) apart. Thread the drapery rings onto the aircraft cable.

2. Attach eye screws into the side walls of a dormer window and attach the aircraft cable with turn buckles to tighten. Clip drapery rings to the folded-over cuff at about 15-inch (38-cm) intervals and hang the fabric. Decorate with a plumb bob if desired.

WARDROBE WIZARDRY

Protect your clothes stylishly with fabric covers.

SHOPPING LIST

- *½ yard (45 cm) of 45-inch (115-cm) quilted fabric for each cover*
- *3 yards (2.8 m) bias binding for each clothes cover*
- *1½ yards (1.4 m) bias binding for each wire hanger cover*
- *thread*

TO MAKE A COVER FOR DUST-FREE CLOTHES: Trace around a wire or wood coat hanger onto a piece of brown paper or newspaper. Then draw another line 1 inch (2.5 cm) outside the first. Cut out around the outer line and use as a pattern. Cut two pieces of quilted fabric for each cover. Cut two pieces of fabric each 2x14½ inches (5 x 36 cm). Machine sew a small hem on one of the short ends of each of these narrow pieces where the hanger neck will poke through. With the wrong sides of fabric together, pin one narrow piece to one long sloped edge of the cover, having the hemmed end at the centre top. Repeat with the second narrow piece, pinning it to the other sloped edge of the same cover piece. Baste in place. Machine stitch bias binding where the pieces are basted together. Attach the remaining cover piece to the other long sides of the thin pieces in the same way. Machine sew bias binding to the lower edge.

TO MAKE A WIRE COAT-HANGER COVERING: Much simpler and faster than a clothes cover, simply trace around a wire coat hanger onto a piece of paper. Draw another line ½ inch (1 cm) outside the first. Cut out around the outside line and use as a pattern. Cut out two pieces of quilted fabric. Machine sew bias binding to the bottom edges. With the right sides of the fabric showing, sew bias binding around the curved edges, joining the two pieces. Leave a hole at the top for the hanger neck to poke through.

FOR HEART-SHAPED SACHETS: Cut two pieces of quilted fabric and machine stitch together with bias binding, leaving a 1-inch (2.5-cm) opening. Fill with scented lavender or potpourri. Slip stitch the opening closed and hand sew a bias-binding loop at the top.

FLOWER-POWER WINDOWS

Découpage a plain rod and rings to glamorize a window covering.

SHOPPING LIST

wooden curtain rod, rings and finials
acrylic paint, if needed to change the
* color of the rod, etc.*
pretty images cut from cards, books or
* magazines*
découpage scissors
white craft glue
high-gloss acrylic varnish

1. Start with a colored wooden rod, rings and finials, or paint a plain set with at least three coats of acrylic paint in a color that will work well with your room's decor, sanding between coats.

2. Cut out small floral images from découpage papers, wrapping paper or magazines.

3. Use craft glue to attach the shapes to the drapery rod and rings. Let dry, then cover with three coats of high-gloss acrylic varnish, allowing to dry between coats.

COVER UP

Fabric-covered storage boxes hold all but tell nothing. They're so pretty they should be on display, not hidden behind closed doors.

SHOPPING LIST

• *heavyweight storage boxes with*
    separate bottoms and lids
• *fabric*
• *white craft glue*
• *hot-glue gun and glue sticks*
• *cord and tassels*

1. Lay the fabric wrong-side up on a flat surface. Set the box bottom in the centre. Lift the fabric up the edges and mark where it reaches the top. Add ½ inch (1 cm) to these marks and use a ruler to draw on the wrong side of the fabric where to cut for the bottom covering.

2. Cut the piece out of the fabric. Set the box in the centre again and on the wrong side of the fabric, draw around its base. Use a ruler to extend the lines of the box outline right out to the edge of the fabric, thus creating four small squares in each corner in addition to the large box shape in the middle of the fabric. Leaving a ½-inch (1-cm) seam allowance, cut the squares out of the four corners. Mitre a slit into each corner seam allowance, ending the slit exactly at the place on the fabric marked as the corner of the box.

3. Press under the seam allowance of the ends. Lay the box back on the wrong side of the fabric and spread a thin line of glue along the upper and end edges of the side pieces of the fabric. Lift up the side pieces and fold the gluey edge to the inside of the top rim of the box. Press the glued-side seam allowance around to the ends of the box.

4. Spread a thin line of glue along the top edge of the end pieces and along the folded-in seam allowance. Lift the fabric up and over the top edge of the box and press in place inside and along the neat edge at the outside ends.

5. Repeat for the lid of the box. When the glue has dried, use a glue gun to attach cord to the edge of the lid and tassels at each corner.

FLOORED WITH FABULOUS FABRIC

Cover floors — and walls — with heavyweight cotton fabric. This treatment works best in a small, narrow room that gets little traffic.

SHOPPING LIST

- ⅝-inch (1.5-cm) plywood cut to fit floor and screwed in place
- Polyfilla
- sandpaper
- heavyweight cotton fabric
- white glue
- 3-inch (8-cm) paintbrush
- polyurethane varnish
- cord or trim (optional)

1. Screw the plywood to the existing floor. Use Polyfilla to cover the screws and to fill any cracks. Let dry, then sand.

2. Cut the fabric to fit, matching the pattern at the edges if joins are required. Use a paintbrush to spread a thin layer of glue along the furthest edge of the floor, in a strip about 10 inches (25 cm) wide. Lower the fabric onto the glue and press firmly in place.

3. Spread another 10-inch (25-cm) wide strip of glue onto the floor, and press the fabric in place. Continue until all the fabric is glued to the plywood. Let dry for 24 hours, then apply a layer of varnish. Let dry, sand lightly, then apply five more coats of varnish sanding between coats. Repeat on the walls if desired.

WINDOW DRESSING

Printed fabrics and romantic frills put a new spin on sheers.

SHOPPING LIST

- enough fabric for 2½ times the window width and appropriate length plus fabric 2½ times the window width and 17 inches (43 cm) deep for the flounce
- lightweight lining for the flounce
- matching thread
- curtain rod and brackets
- matching tassels

1. Sew the fabric pieces together to form a covering that is 2½ times as wide as the window and long enough that it puddles on the floor. Machine stitch a 1-inch (2.5-cm) double hem along the curtain edges. Turn under the fabric at the bottom edge, 3 inches (8 cm), twice. Press, then machine stitch.

2. Sew the panels together for the flounce. Cut a paper pattern with 15-inch (38-cm) deep points. Use this pattern to cut out the bottom edge of the flounce fabric and matching lining fabric. The flounce and its lining should be 17 inches (43 cm) deep. With right sides of the flounce fabric and lining pinned together, sew along the pointed edge. Clip V angles between the points, turn right-side out and press.

3. Pin the right side of the flounce to the right side of the top of the curtain. Sew a ¾-inch (2-cm) seam along the top edge, through all the layers. Flip the flounce over to the back of the curtain and sew another seam to create a pocket wide enough to accommodate the rod. Flip the flounce back to the front and sew tassles at each point. Thread the rod through the pocket and mount.

OUTDOOR

ROOMS

MOVING OUT
Summertime . . . and the living is outdoors,
especially when the outdoor room is as
snoozing-in-the-shade comfy as this one.
Handsome twig furniture — chairs softened by
cushions, a tiered stand laden with dishes and
books — creates a country feeling at the back of
a city house. A basket full of magazines and a
chair-side table for iced tea make this room the
perfect setting for easy, no-effort relaxing.

GORGEOUS LIVING-ROOM GARDENS

VICTORIAN GENTILITY
Balmy breezes blow gently through the lattice panels of a covered porch. Framed and painted forest green, the lattice insets screen out both traffic noise and the curiosity of pedestrian passersby. In a setting reminiscent of the Victorian times when the house was built, dark wicker furniture set on a tomato-red floor invites an afternoon of delectable conversation and homemade lemonade.

WHEN THE SUN shines and the temperature climbs to soul-replenishing heights, the desire to remain indoors disappears as quickly as drops of rain on a hot pavement. Seekers of comfort that we are, however, we are not prepared to relinquish any of the luxuries we demand — and have — indoors, simply because we decide to move outdoors during warm summer months.

Outdoor living means comfortable chairs, tables close-by for books and drinks, lighting adequate for a variety of needs, just as in indoor living rooms, plus shelter from sweltering sun at the height of the day. The challenge, then, is to combine the charm of the out-of-doors with the comforts of indoors.

Pursuing a course of take-it-easy decorating, the outdoor living room can be created on a covered porch, where trellised walls capture balmy breezes (see opposite), on a projecting deck, where access to the indoors is a step away, on a high-rise balcony (page 89) or a landscaped rooftop (see page 92), or arranged on the grass under the shade of a glade of trees.

All the furniture in an outdoor room should be weather friendly, able to withstand scorching sun or pelting rain. Some natural materials are ideal for this. Twig furniture (see Rustic Garden Bench, pages 99 to 101) can withstand any weather that nature tosses its way; some types of wrought-iron or aluminum furniture can also be left to the elements with no fear of damage; the relatively new resin tables and

ALL DECKED OUT

A cedar deck cantilevered into a ravine offers lots of
options: dine at the table, pull out the lounge chairs or
sink into a hammock strung between cherry and chestnut
trees that rim the edge of the deck. Light enough to
relocate, the furniture follows the sun or shade
throughout the day. Ceramic pots of flowers and an old
farm cart brimming with blossoms accessorize the space.

chairs, manufactured in many colors, withstand everything but frost with equanimity, and require only the touch of a cloth to dry off water or sweep away dust.

Chairs need not be less comfortable than indoors; in fact, because they are used in a decidedly casual setting, they can be oversized, plumped with sink-into pillows, which are covered with all-weather fabric — so a night in the rain will not ruin their stuffing — and accompanied by matching footstools if desired. And for the ultimate in outdoor relaxation, don't forget the charms of a hammock! Remember: the primary activity in an outdoor living room is resting and relaxing with your feet up enjoying the best that summer offers! 🌿

WATER MUSIC
A wall-mounted terra-cotta fountain peeks from behind greenery clambering up an arch-shaped trellis in a formal outdoor arrangement. Styrofoam panels lining the planters protect the hardy perennial vines, such as Boston ivy and clematis, from harsh winter weather.

TREETOP LIVING

Indoor comfort moves outdoors onto the roof of an apartment building, creating a living space that gets a high satisfaction rating from the family pets. A lattice wall separates a dining area from the living zone; cedar decking tops the pea-gravel surfacing and provides drainage when it rains. Woodsy furniture made from fallen birch logs gets its comfort-quotient raised with all-weather cushions. Pots of flowers and geranium-filled planters along the parapet add color and texture.

QUIET CORNER

Tucked into the corner of an intimate deck, a shaded built-in bench piled with colorful fuss-free, rain-resistent cushions takes up little space but seats four with their feet on the floor or welcomes two stretched out. The garden-furniture designs of Sir Edwin Lutyens, an early 20th-century English architect, inform the curved wooden back-and-arms detail attached to the fence and painted the same color.

HIGH-RISE OASIS

The cozy balcony of a high-rise condo is so sheltered and protected that it's a favorite spot for early-morning coffee and late-night stargazing throughout much of the year. Decorated with accessories reminiscent of an indoor conservatory, the outdoor room's narrow trellis paneling attached to one wall provides a surface for hanging botanical prints. A canvas curtain softens the concrete; all-weather carpeting covers the floor. Wicker furniture topped with sprightly cushions and assorted potted plants, including a robust Norfolk pine, define a small space as a room to escape to.

THROUGH THE GARDEN GATE
In the warm summer months, the front courtyard of a downtown house turns into a second living room. Raised garden beds meander around the perimeter of the tiny yard. Potted plants and tailored shrubs add both color and height. A trellised arbor shades the garden bench cosseted beneath it; moveable antique metal chairs make for flexible seating arrangements.

GARAGE-TOP GARDEN ROOM
Summertime cocktail parties stretch far
into the night when friends gather on a
garage rooftop. Surrounding trees create
a wall of privacy; guests perch on the deep
planters rimming the roof. A pair of
weeping pea shrubs towers over the
outdoor room; flowers in pots set on the
street-side parapet edge bloom profusely.
All the other plants are edible, providing
the household with raspberries, broccoli,
cabbages, eggplant, kohlrabi, onions, garlic,
nasturtiums and more than a dozen herbs.

ROOFTOP JUNGLE
A projecting pergola casts shade over
the verdant outdoor room atop a city
townhouse. Mature apple trees and a
riot of rhododendrons jostle for space
atop a townhouse, whose enveloping
charm — and distant vistas —
encourage sitting and sipping all day
long. Portable chairs and assorted
tables scattered throughout the paths
that wind among the colorful flowers,
large shrubs and fruit-laden trees invite
guests to linger in the intimate "room."

LOUNGE LIVING

Evergreen shrubs, architectural elements and a privacy-creating fence turn the penthouse deck of a high-rise apartment into a secluded outdoor living room. A profusion of plants and an assortment of vines turn the sheltered space into a luxurious resort. With its west-facing aspect, the room enjoys long shadows created by the evening sun. Earlier in the day, a market umbrella and projecting roof above provide respite from the heat.

BRIDGE VIEW

Colorful flowers, that change with the seasons, create a "wall" along an outdoor room that runs the length of a city-centre condominium. Hardy petunias, dusty miller and calendulas toss about in the breeze. Lightweight deck chairs fold up when not being used to watch the action on the bridge and the spectacular skyline beyond the flowering hedge.

ARCHED ARBOR

Delicate passion flowers bloom on the vines that cover the metal archway on a rooftop room. It leads nowhere, but the arch acts like the window in a room, framing the city sights in the distance. Beneath and beside it, concrete planters filled with verbena and cascading geraniums brighten the scene.

Fresh-Air Living
PROJECTS

PAINTING A NEW CANVAS

Look what paint and fabric can do if sun and rain have ruined a canvas chair.

SHOPPING LIST
- about 2 yards (180 cm) heavyweight canvas
- thread
- white matte latex paint
- colored matte latex paint
- exterior house paint for chair frame
- acrylic varnish
- 1-inch (2.5-cm) paintbrush
- fine-grit sandpaper

1. Carefully inspect how the fabric is attached to the chair, then remove it and use as a pattern.

2. Prepare the fabric: paint with one coat of white latex paint. Set aside to dry. (It will shrink.)

3. Lay the original cover on top of the prepared canvas and cut out a new piece, adding 1 inch (2.5 cm) to the width and 4 inches (10 cm) to the length for hems. Overcast the raw edges to prevent fraying.

4. Press and machine stitch a ½-inch (1-cm) hem on both long sides. Press and machine-stitch hems along the top and bottom edges to make a new seat the same size as the original.

5. Mark out a checkerboard pattern, then paint. Let dry. Apply one coat of acrylic varnish.

6. Sand the chair frame well, then paint with two coats of exterior house paint. Attach the canvas, as it was originally, to the chair's frame.

MUSKOKA CHAIR MAKEOVER

Pretty up a plain Muskoka chair with a stencil.

SHOPPING LIST
- fine- and medium-grit sandpaper
- oil-based paint
- stencil
- stencil brushes
- stensil adhesive spray
- oil-based varnish

1. Sand new wood with fine sandpaper. If the chair is worn, sand well with medium-grit sandpaper to smooth the surface.

2. New wood can be left bare, or painted with three coats of oil-based paint.

3. Attach the stencil to chair with a spray stencil adhesive. Apply the design using a brush and oil-based paint. Let dry. Apply three coats of oil-based varnish, sanding between coats.

RUSTIC GARDEN BENCH

Twig, or "tree," furniture is a natural for a garden room, whether you keep it in the backyard or the dining room. This bench was made with cedar, an excellent no-maintenance choice for outdoors.

(Instructions overleaf)

DO-IT-YOURSELF

RUSTIC GARDEN BENCH

SHOPPING LIST

Note: The first number given in the measurement is the diameter. For example, two 2 x 16-inch pieces means 2 branches approximately 2 inches in diameter and 16 inches long.

- *two 2 x 16-inch pieces for front legs*
- *two 2 x 24-inch pieces for back legs*
- *four 1½ x 36-inch pieces for front and back rails*
- *four 1½ x 24-inch pieces for side rails*
- *two 1 x 24-inch pieces for braces (you will cut to size during construction)*
- *20 1-inch branches (to be used for decorating the front and back seating)*
- *ardox finishing nails (a selection from 1 inch to 4 inches — come in ½-inch increments)*
- *1 box 1-inch brown panelling nails*
- *1 box 1⅝-inch brown panelling nails*
- *orange shellac*
- *small brush*

TOOLS

- *bow (camp) saw*
- *pair of long-handled garden snips*
- *garden shears*
- *utility knife*
- *tape measure*
- *hammer*
- *file or hacksaw*

1. Prepare the 2 front legs, 2 back legs, and 8 rails specified. Use a utility knife to carve a 45-degree slant on each end of each of these 12 pieces, which will help to keep the bark from unraveling.

Lay out side Frame A on a table (see Figure 1). Place the back leg on the table corner as shown. Position the front leg so that the top side rail when put in place extends 2 inches past each leg and 2 inches down from the top of the front leg. Tack the rail in place with an appropriately sized ardox-finishing nail.

Measure the distance from the underside of the top rail to the bottom of the front leg. Position the top rail so that it drops 2 inches on the back leg and extends 2 inches past. Tack it in place with a nail.

Be sure to keep the bottoms of both legs lined up with the edge of the table. This will insure that when you stand the frame up it will be correctly aligned.

Position the bottom rail 3 inches up from the bottom of both legs and have it extend 2 inches past the front leg.

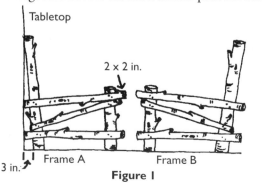

Tabletop

2 x 2 in.

3 in.

Frame A   Frame B

Figure 1

Tack it in place on both legs. It will extend more than 2 inches past the back leg because of the angle that leg will be on. Now stand Frame A on the table and check that, when the front leg is straight up and down in front of you, the back leg is on a comfortable-looking angle, the top seat rail is sloping down towards the back, and the bottom rail appears level.

If everything checks out, lay it back down on the corner of the table, making sure the bottoms of the legs line up with the table edge. Take one of the 24-inch braces and nail to the frame as shown in Figure 1. You can now double nail each rail to the legs as well as the brace.

2. With Frame A repositioned on the table corner lay out Frame B next to it exactly the same way, but reversed.

Repeat Step 1 to produce Frame B. When you are done, stand both frames upright on the table and make sure that they are mirror images of each other.

3. Join the side frames by nailing the remaining front and back rails (36 inches). Arrange the two side frames on the table edge as shown in Figure 2. The frame rails should be to the outside and the top of the front legs "hooked" on the table. Tack the top front rail to the legs so that it comes flush with the outside of the side rails. Take note that these remaining 4 rails are all positioned on top of the side rails. Next rotate everything 180 degrees until the bottoms of the front legs are "hooked" and your stomach is against the top front rail and

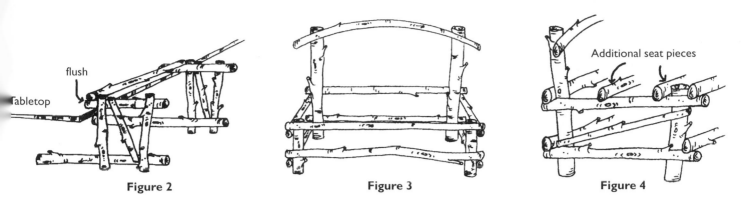

Figure 2   Figure 3   Figure 4

holding everything against the table. Tack the bottom front rail as you did the top. Stand the frame on the top of the table and see if both front rails are level and the front legs are straight up and down.

Leave the frame standing on the table and from behind tack the top back rail on top of the side rails and to the back legs. Leave an overhang of 1½ inches past the outside of the side rails. This overhang will make the back narrower than the front. Tack the bottom back rail to the legs and on top of the side rails with the same 1½-inch overhang.

If the frame looks all right from both the front and back views, double nail the front and back rails. Now, add a top arch to the back legs. Choose a branch that is between 1 and 1½ inches for this and cut it on either side of the back legs after it is nailed in place. Leave an overhang of about 3 inches on both sides. See Figure 3.

4. Nail on two final seat pieces. These should be 36 inches long, the same diameter and shape as the top front rail, and placed as shown in Figure 4. The intent is to have a fairly flat upper surface to sit on.

5. Add front and back decorative pieces (see Figure 5). The pieces in Figure 5 that are labeled "Brace" are very important and should be at least 1 inch in diameter, because they will lock the legs in place. Nail the arms in place as shown in Figure 6. The arm branches should be approximately 2 inches in diameter. Double nail them to the back legs, the front legs and, if possible, to a frame seat member as well.

6. Finish off the seat. These pieces should be each about ¾ inch in diameter and reasonably straight. Figure 7 shows a typical seat layout. Start with the seat header — which is the dark piece in Figure 7. Nail it directly down onto the seat rail. The reason for this seat header is to cover the exposed ends of the seat pieces and to allow you to nail through the header into the ends of the seat pieces.

The nailing will start at the seat rail behind the front legs and the second nail will be into the middle rail. Leave the nailing at the back rail for now and use brown 1⅝-inch panel nails if they're long enough, otherwise use a larger ardox-finishing nail. Place them in the order shown in Figure 7, working alternately from the inside of the legs towards the middle with a spacing of about 1 inch between branches. Adjust the spacing as needed in order to end up with a visually pleasing pattern. Now nail them down onto the back rail. Finish off with 1 or 2 shorter pieces on each side. Add the curved branch that goes behind the back legs and on top of the seat.

7. Apply orange shellac to anyplace the bark is broken, such as cut ends or branches. This process allows the moisture that leaves the wood during seasoning to evaporate through the bark so the wood and bark dry at the same rate.

Note: Other woods that are good to use for this bench if you plan to keep it indoors include willow and tag alder. These woods require a coat of MinWax Protective Antique Oil, applied with a nozzle spray bottle.

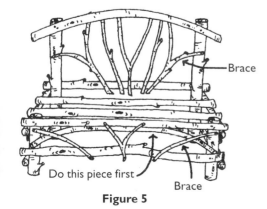

Figure 5

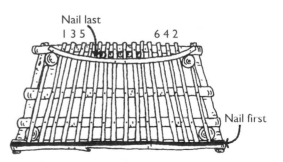

Figure 6

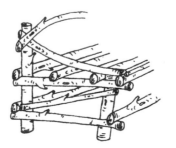

Figure 7

WINDOW BOX

This window box looks elegant, but it is easy to make because there's no tricky joinery. Essentially, it's a simple plywood box, strong enough for a generous array of plants, clad with attractive tongue-and-groove cedar and trimmed at the top and bottom with mitred cedar corner moldings.

Note: Measurements result in a window box 39 inches long, 11 inches wide and 9 inches deep. Adjust to fit your own windows.

SHOPPING LIST

- *½-inch fir plywood, 48x48 inches*
- *three 1 x 2-inch strips of wood, each 6 feet long*
- *four pieces ½ x 4-inch clear (no knots) tongue-and-groove cedar, each 6 feet long*
- *50 1-inch wood screws*
- *½ lb (250 g) 1¼-inch galvanized finishing nails*
- *2 pieces cedar corner molding for top and bottom trim, each 6 feet long*
- *wood filler*
- *sandpaper*
- *oil-based stain (optional)*

TOOLS

- *circular or table saw*
- *2 C-clamps*
- *electric or cordless drill with screwdriver attachment*
- *¾-inch drill bit*
- *handsaw*
- *mitre box and coping saw*
- *hammer*
- *nail set (punch)*
- *pencil*

Method for making the box

1. Cut the bottom piece, 9x37 inches, from the plywood.

2. Cut two pieces, each 8½ x 38 inches, from the plywood.

3. Cut two 9x8½-inch pieces from the plywood for the ends.

4. To make cleats (interior supporting pieces), cut 1 x 2-inch wood into four pieces 34 inches, four pieces 7½ inches, and four pieces 7 inches long.

5. Drill 12 evenly spaced holes ¾ inch in diameter through the bottom for drainage. (If using a plastic liner, line up the holes with the liner's drainage holes.)

6. Using C-clamps, clamp two of the 34-inch and two of the 7½-inch cleats to the bottom piece, placing cleats on their ends, flush to the edges of the bottom piece, leaving space for corner cleats to fit snugly. Turn the end piece over and screw the cleats on from the bottom.

8. Place the end piece in position, again covering the cut edge of bottom piece, and screw into the cleat. Repeat with the other end piece.

9. Clamp one 34-inch cleat into position on the inside of the back, 1 inch from the top, and screw from the outside of the plywood; repeat with the front cleat. Repeat with 7½-inch cleats at the end.

10. Drop the 7-inch corner cleats into position and secure the corners, using four screws for each corner, two at the back and front, and two at each side, screwing into the cleats, not into the plywood.

To apply tongue-and-groove and trim molding

1. Use a handsaw to cut tongue-and-groove cedar into 33 pieces, each 8½ inches long.

2. Turn the box on its back and place the cedar pieces in position on the front, centring them (12 complete pieces fit onto the front and the back). Cut one piece of cedar lengthwise into two pieces each 1 inch wide — one from the tongue side, one from the groove side—to finish the front.

3. Mark a pencil line at the right to indicate the placement of the first tongue-and-groove piece; place the groove-side right and the tongue-side left. Nail into place through the tongue, using two finishing nails. With a nail set, countersink the nails. Place the next groove piece over the tongue and nail into place, continuing until the front is covered. Nail the two partial pieces into place to complete the front. Repeat with the ends and the back of the window box.

4. Cut four corner molding trim pieces 40 inches long (for the front and back, bottom and top), and four trim pieces 12 inches long (for the ends, bottom and top). Mitre 45 degrees at the corners and nail onto the top of the box with finishing nails; sink the nails with a nail set. Turn the box over and trim the bottom in the same fashion.

5. Fill the nail holes with wood filler, sand off any excess. Sand any rough edges before staining.

For planting tips, see Container Gardening *next page.*

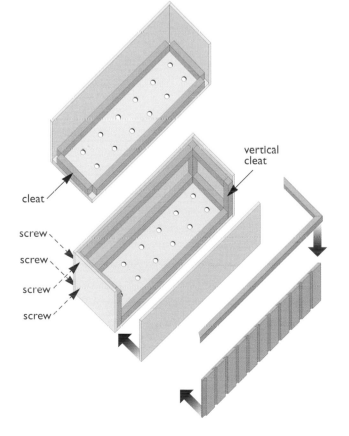

cleat

vertical cleat

screw

screw

screw

screw

TIPS

- While a cedar-clad box can be left to "weather" naturally, turning a pleasant gray shade with time, it will last longer if stained. By staining you can match the color of your box to your deck or house.

- To increase the longevity of a box, insert a plastic liner to hold the soil and plants.

- A large window box is heavy, so be sure to attach it to the house using strong decorative brackets and properly anchored bolts, available at hardware stores and lumberyards.

- To keep the box as light as possible, use a potting soil or container mix (not garden or topsoil), which contains lightweight moisture-absorbent crystals that slowly release water.

CONTAINER GARDENING

Anytime is a great time to fill your garden, patio or deck with pots filled with flowers and plants, so don't be contained by the weather. Here are some tips to keep patios and balconies looking great all year long.

SUMMERTIME CONTAINER PLANTS

Almost any flowering annual plant will grow in a container. Some of the best choices are geraniums, petunias, abutilon, verbena, lobelia, nasturtiums, marigolds, impatiens and scaevola.

Containers

Window boxes, clay pots and old wheelbarrows all make great containers for summertime plants. The bigger the container the happier the plants will be, because larger containers take longer to dry out. Containers made of porous materials, such as clay and wood, are best because they "breathe."

Growing tips

Use a good all-purpose potting soil, available at nurseries. Plant densely. In a 10-inch (25-cm) container, for instance, use at least five plants. The plants will quickly cover the surface and spill over the sides, covering the pot.

Fill the pot almost to the top with soil, tamp it down lightly and moisten. Then make small holes for the flower's root system. Once the roots are inserted, gently firm the soil around them. Water the plants with a water-soluble transplant fertilizer.

Water whenever the surface of the soil is dry to the touch. Check the moisture levels every day in summer — severe wilting will reduce the flowering of many plants. Water-soluble fertilizer should be applied every fifth watering. Either 15-30-15 or 20-20-20 works well.

Do a little light pruning to keep new growth coming from the base of the plants. Once a week, remove all the dead blooms.

YEAR-ROUND CONTAINER PLANTS

While pots of annuals end with summer, container-grown trees and shrubs will survive most winters and thrive for years if properly planted and cared for.

Selecting plants

Hardiness is the chief consideration in choosing trees and shrubs for container growing. Before you buy, check the hardiness zone rating — the lower the rating, the more cold-hardy the plant — and always choose those rated for two zones colder than your area. Go to your local garden centre for advice about zone ratings. Make certain that your container size and the plants you select are appropriate to withstand your winter conditions.

Container plants should remain fairly short, so they don't overgrow the pot in a few years. Dwarf trees, flowering shrubs, vines and low-growing evergreens all work well.

Some suggestions: evergreens such as emerald cedar, upright and spreading junipers and globe blue spruce; flowering shrubs such as silverleaf dogwood, purple-leaf sandcherry, lilac and dwarf burning bush; dwarf trees such as standard flowering almond, weeping caragana, Amur maple and red jade weeping crab apple; vines such as Virginia creeper, bittersweet and clematis virginiana.

Containers

The bigger the better. Small containers tend to freeze and thaw as the weather fluctuates. Big containers are often difficult to find, so consider building your own (see Window Box pages 102 and 103). All containers should have drainage holes.

Growing tips

Use a soil mixture of two parts weed-free topsoil and one part peat moss. Top-dress the containers with 2 inches (5 cm) shredded cedar mulch.

Plant by mid-July at the latest, so that the root system is well established before the onslaught of cold weather.

Apply a water-soluble fertilizer (15-30-15 or 20-20-20 for deciduous plants and 30-10-10 for evergreens) every three weeks from spring until mid-August. Never fertilize beyond this point.

Complete all pruning and trimming before mid-August.

Never allow container-grown plants to wilt severely. Water thoroughly up to three times a week in the hottest part of the summer. Even in the fall, check the moisture levels to ensure that the plants will be damp going into the winter. Generally, watering is not necessary throughout the winter unless there is a thaw.

Dining Alfresco
GOING OUT FOR DINNER

$\mathcal{D}$INING OUTDOORS in warm weather prolongs the enjoyment of every meal of the day, but to make it happen easily requires some preliminary attention to details.

Until the sun goes down in the evening sky, shade is of primary importance. Covered porches provide the best protection from the sun, as the dining room opposite reveals, but canvas market umbrellas also do the trick with style and effectiveness, covering a relatively large area without closing off too much light.

Shade-creating pergolas made from slats of wood or vine-covered arbors (see page 111) block out the bulk of the sun's rays but filter the light through in a dappled fashion and permit gentle breezes to cool the diners seated beneath. They can easily be strung with twinkling miniature lights or with amusing shapes for a whimsical effect at night.

Because we tend to linger longer at the outdoor table, which may be made of glass and metal, resin or wood, chairs benefit from cushioned seats. Placemats whose colors match the flowers in the garden or cloths anchored against breezes by knotted corners, decorative clamps or creative weights (see Weighty Subjects, page 117) brighten even the simplest table. Elegance reigns when the table is covered with a damask cloth, more likely found in a formal dining room than out-of-doors (see pages 111 to 113). And to protect candles from flickering out or splashing wax, glass hurricane-lamp covers both shield flames and add decorative touches to the alfresco table (see Glass Acts, page 121).

RUSTIC REPASTS
In the warm summer months, everybody moves outdoors to a sheltered family dining room, but when there's a party planned, the room really comes to life. Candles flicker in the chandelier, whose glass cups provide protection from breezes; large hurricane-lamp covers shield chunky candles on the twig table. An ironstone jug holds a cluster of casual flowers; collectable vintage Jade-ite dishes match the fringed tablecloth. In keeping with the rustic theme, a napkin-lined basket holds cutlery and an old metal milk-bottle carrier totes assorted condiments and serving pieces between the porch and the kitchen.

A wrought-iron and glass table set with pretty pink accessories creates a summery mood on the deck. All-weather cushions give comfort to the matching chairs, encouraging dinner guests to relax through leisurely meals served on delicately decorated Italian chinaware. A tall fence provides privacy; a metal serving table holds extra dishes.

The surrounding garden provides everything required for plain and simple or more adventuresome and elaborate table centrepieces. Fruits and vegetables are as interesting as flowers and leaves; combinations of all these elements make a colorful display for dinner-table guests.

The food can be served on plates that are funky or on fine bone china. Cutlery can range from the family silver to mismatched camping pieces. Always keep in mind that the object of dining outdoors is to create an atmosphere of laid-back relaxation, where anything goes, and those who gather there enjoy themselves to the fullest. ✄

UNDERNEATH THE ARBOR

A hint of irony creeps into an otherwise glamorous setting, where outdoor dining includes fine linens and fringed tapestry, branched candelabra and silver cutlery. It's the neighbor's laundry blowing in the breeze and hubcaps decorating the wall of an adjacent garage that keep the scene from becoming overly serious. A sheltering arbor of grapes and kiwi strung with fanciful fish lights creates a feeling of intimacy, setting the dining room apart from all worldly intrusions.

SUMMERY SUPPER SETTING

The late-evening sun warms a dining room set for a casual supper outdoors. Clear glass plates, candle holders and stemware on the table feel cool and summery. A silver-lace vine softens the pillar supporting the trellised roof. Cedar hedges underplanted with colorful impatiens fill railing-side planters.

FINE DINING

Dinner in the garden takes on all the formality and graciousness of dining indoors when the fine linens, crystal and silverware are simply moved outdoors. And why not? With the stars overhead and the fragrance of flowers nearby, a warm summer evening in the garden becomes a memorable magical experience. Small bouquets of tiny flowers and bowls of fruit are all it takes to embellish the linen-draped table.

FANTASY DINING
Colorful sari fabrics and flickering candles transform a harborside high-rise balcony into an intimate dining den, suggestive of an evening in a mysterious "Sultan's tent". Jewel-toned saris — strung with wire from the balcony above and draped over a small table and wrapped around chairs — sparkle in the twinkling light of tiny hanging oil lamps and covered lanterns. Glittering Indian bracelets turn into inexpensive napkin rings. Tall reeds plucked from a country road-side, piles of pillows on the floor and a small richly patterned carpet add more layers of mystery.

PERGOLA PARTY
Colorful accessories decorate a dining scene set beneath a small cupola attached to a suburban house. An eclectic mix of styles from funky to chic give the outdoor room a unique vibrance. A cast-iron cow hibachi stands firmly atop a massive log. Limestone slabs, gathered on the shores of Georgian Bay, make unique serving plates. The centrepiece — a flower-strewn ice bowl — cools down the hot summer temperature and chills bottled water. Its shimmery surface repeats the iridescent sheen of the fabric that decks out the chairs in party dresses.

Dining Alfresco
PROJECTS

NOVEL NAPKIN RINGS

Capture the essence of the garden with easy-to-make napkin holders.

SHOPPING LIST

FOR ROSE RINGS
- *plaster of Paris*
- *flexible candy molds shaped like roses or other flowers*
- *2-inch (5-cm) diameter brass café-curtain rings*
- *fine sandpaper*
- *1 (2 fl oz/59 mL) bottle acrylic craft paint in pink, red and green*
- *small artist's brush*
- *1 (2 fl oz/59 mL) bottle acrylic craft varnish*

FOR WREATH RINGS
- *miniature vine wreaths*
- *hot-glue gun and glue sticks*
- *tiny fabric flowers and leaves, miniature birds and birds' nests*

Rose Rings

1. Mix a small amount of plaster of Paris with water until it has the consistency of very thick cream or batter. Pour it into candy molds. Smooth the surface.

2. Dip the shank part of the ring, which would be sewn to the curtain, into the centre of each mold. If the plaster is sufficiently thick, the ring will stand upright on its own. If the plaster is too thin, thread the ring onto a bamboo skewer or chopstick and rest it on a small cup at each end so the ring is held firmly upright in position. Let the plaster dry for about 4 hours. Pop from the molds. Smooth any rough edges, using sandpaper.

3. Paint the flowers and leaves as desired. Set aside to dry, then paint with one coat of varnish.

Wreath Rings

1. Check out craft stores for all the supplies you need to make these prettily decorated vine wreaths.

2. If the flowers are sold in clusters, break the bunches apart, cut the wire or plastic stems very short and glue to the wreath.

3. Use a glue gun to attach miniature birds in the tiny nest.

WALL HANGING

Hanging baskets filled with flowering plants put color on outdoor dining-room walls.

> ### SHOPPING LIST
> - a wall-mounted wire or wicker basket
> - sheet moss
> - potting soil
> - flowering plants

1. Line the sides and bottom of a wire or wicker planter with sheet moss. Add a small amount of potting soil.

2. Transfer small pots of flowering plants from their containers to the planter. Add more soil, pressing down to fill in any spaces.

3. Hang on an outdoor wall for instant decoration. Water as required. Add new plants as the seasons change.

WEIGHTY SUBJECTS

Decorative weights keep tablecloths from blowing in the breeze.

> ### SHOPPING LIST
> - a selection of colored polymer clays by manufacturers such as Sculpey or Fimo
> - polymer-clay glaze
> - small beads
> - thin wire
> - hot-glue gun and glue sticks
> - needle and thread

1. Mold polymer clay into shapes that are inspired by the patterns in your tablecloth(s). Make shapes about 1½ inches (4 cm) in diameter and create enough to sew about 10 inches (25 cm) apart along the bottom edges of a cloth.

2. Bake according to manufacturer's instructions. Let cool, then apply one coat of glaze.

3. Thread one or two beads onto thin wire and bend into a loop. Use a hot-glue gun to attach the wire to the back of each weight.

4. Sew to the cloth using matching thread.

SHOPPING LIST

FRAME
- (2 upright,* 3 cross members)
- three 10-foot 2x4 boards, pressure-treated or cedar; cut one of these pieces into three 36-inch sections

TOP LATTICE
- one 1x8-foot diagonal lattice (comes ready-made), pressure-treated or cedar; cut to symmetrical 36-inch length

BOTTOM LATTICE
- two 8-foot 2x6 boards, ripped into 1x2 lengths; from these, cut five 50-inch and seven 36-inch lengths**

NAILING STRIPS
- six 8-foot lengths

FASTENERS
- ½ lb (250 g) 1¼-inch galvanized finishing nails
- 12 3-inch No. 10 chrome-plated screws for frame
- 35 1¼-inch No. 8 chrome-plated screws for square lattice
- 4 2½-inch No. 10 chrome-plated screws for fence-post caps

ACCESSORIES
- 2 beveled fence-post caps; 2 fence-post finials
- 1 quart (1 L) oil-based stain (optional)

*Use 10-foot 2x4s as support pieces only if you are building a freestanding trellis to be set into concrete footings. If your trellis is to be attached to a wall, use 6½-foot 2x4s as supports.

**If available, buy 1x2 lumber. Many lumberyards do not carry it, but will rip wood into 1x2s for a nominal charge.

TOOLS
- measuring tape
- hammer
- handsaw
- screwdriver (or drill with screwdriver attachment)
- drill with 3/16 and 11/64 bits

GARDEN TRELLIS

Trellises, together with lush climbing vines, are among the most decorative and practical of garden ornaments. As well as giving structure and height to a garden, an attractive trellis will dress up bare exterior walls and help define "garden rooms."

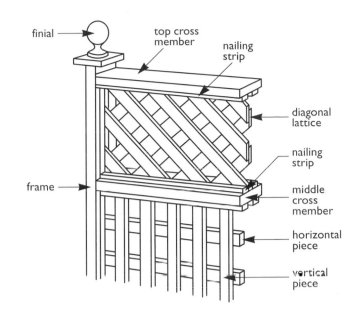

To make the frame

1. On a flat surface, place two 10-foot 2 x 4s parallel on edge, 36 inches apart. Position the first 36-inch cross member on edge between the uprights, 3 inches from the top. Attach with two 3-inch No. 10 screws through each upright to secure horizontally.

2. The second cross member goes exactly 12 inches below the first one, allowing proper spacing for the diagonal trellis panel; secure as above.

3. Place the third cross member 50 inches down from the second one and secure as above.

Top diagonal lattice

1. The lattice is held in place by a nailing strip frame behind and in front. Do not nail through the lattice. Cut nailing strip pieces to size; four pieces 10¾ inches long; four pieces 36 inches long. The object is to end up with lattice centred in the 12 x 36-inch frame. Therefore, set the first 36-inch nailing strip about 1 inch from the bottom edge of the 2 x 4 frame. Nail in place with finishing nails. Nail the second horizontal nailing strip into the frame, followed by the two vertical 10¾-inch strips.

2. Then drop the diagonal lattice panel into place on top of the nailing strip frame; set remaining nailing strips into place on the top of the lattice and nail each into the 2 x 4 frame.

Bottom square lattice

1. Cut four 50-inch nailing strips and four 36-inch nailing strips.

2. To support the seven 36-inch horizontal lattice pieces, set two of the 50-inch nailing strips onto the inside frame about ½ inch from the bottom edge of 2 x 4 and secure with finishing nails.

3. Place the seven horizontal lattice pieces into place, spacing them 4½ inches apart, and nail the ends into the nailing strips.

4. Set the top and bottom 36-inch nailing strips into place, so that their ends overlap the ends of the vertical nailing strips, and nail into the 2 x 4 frame.

5. Set the five vertical 50-inch lattice pieces on top of the horizontals 4½ inches apart and nail the ends into the nailing strip.

6. Set the remaining two vertical nailing strips into place, covering the nailed ends of the horizontal lattice pieces, and nail into the 2 x 4 frame. Do the same with the last two horizontal nailing strips, overlapping the ends of the vertical nailing strips at the top and bottom.

7. To finish, screw the lattice together at intersecting points from the back so the screws won't show, using No. 8 screws. To prevent the wood splitting, predrill the holes with an ¹¹⁄₆₄ bit.

Cap, finial and finishing

1. Centre the caps on top of the 2 x 4 uprights and secure with 2 ½-inch No. 10 screws. Predrill the holes with ³⁄₁₆ bit.

2. Screw the finial into place at the centre of each cap. (Finials come fitted with screws.)

3. For added durability, stain the trellis with a semi-transparent or opaque exterior oil-based wood stain.

Installation

1. To install a freestanding trellis, dig post holes 3 feet deep using a fence-post digger. Place 3 inches of gravel in the bottom of the holes and tamp down. Set and level the trellis in the holes, and pour in concrete. Smooth the concrete so the water flows away from the wood.

2. To install against a wall, use metal brackets or wood as spacers, and leave 3 to 5 inches of space between the trellis and the wall for air circulation. Set the feet of the trellis on bricks or stone to avoid contact with damp soil and to prevent wood decay.

PICNIC TABLE PERK UP

Don't pay big bucks for a fancy picnic table. With a little creativity, ingenuity and elbow grease, you can turn a hardware-store basic into a backyard beauty.

SHOPPING LIST

- *picnic table*
- *router (with Classic Roman Ogee bit)*
- *sandpaper*
- *electric jigsaw*
- *latex primer paint*
- *exterior oil-based paint*
- *4-inch (10-cm) paintbrush*

1. Using a router fitted with a Classic Roman Ogee bit, shave off the edges of the tabletop and bench seats to give them a finished look. Sand to smooth any rough edges.

2. Decide on a design for custom cutouts. This table has an apple shape which was drawn on a piece of cardboard and used as a template for tracing onto the tabletop.

3. Using an electric jigsaw, cut out as many shapes as you want from the tabletop. Sand any rough edges.

4. Using latex primer, paint the entire table including the insides of the cutouts. Use exterior oil-based paint on the whole table, choosing a different color for the insides of the cutouts if you wish. Let dry, then repeat with a second coat of paint.

GLASS ACTS

Decorate a plain hurricane-lamp shade with glass etching.

SHOPPING LIST

- *glass hurricane-lamp shade*
- *rub-on glass etching stencil*
- *flat wooden stick (or discarded popsicle stick)*
- *¼-inch (5-mm) paintbrush with stiff bristles*
- *etching medium*
- *rubber or latex gloves*

1. Clean the hurricane glass well and dry thoroughly. Apply the stencil to the outside of the glass following the directions on the package. (A flat wooden stick rubbed over the surface of the stencil works well.)

2. Use a small stiff paintbrush to apply a thick coat of etching medium to the cutout portions of the stencil. Do not get any drops of medium elsewhere on the glass. Wait for five minutes or the length of time specified on the etching medium.

3. Wear rubber gloves. Hold the hurricane glass under warm running water and rub off the stencil. The etched portion will remain on the glass.

DO-IT-YOURSELF

VINES GROW UP

Vines can disguise bland fences, ugly garages and drab walls, often with breathtaking masses of color. And when they're trained up arbors and trellises, they can create islands of privacy in a yard or on a balcony. Here's how to set them up.

Walls

Nonflowering self-adhering vines, such as Boston ivy, can simply be planted at the base of masonry walls and allowed to climb.

Flowering vines, such as climbing roses and clematis, are by far the most popular because of their spectacular blooms. Like all other nonadhering vines, they must be supported by trellises. Cedar or redwood trellises are good choices because of their durability. Fasten them securely to the wall.

Fences

Use the same type of vine along the entire stretch of a fence. This avoids different vines competing with each other or having to be continually pruned in order to keep them separate.

Most vines planted about 4 to 5 feet (120 to 150 cm) apart will give solid cover for a fence. They should have at least a 14-inch (35-cm) wide bed to grow in.

Arbors

Discover the joys of a secluded arbor. At their simplest, arbors consist of wooden posts mounted on concrete footings. The posts are placed around the perimeter of the arbor, and the "walls" between the posts are enclosed with wood lattice. Leave one or more sections of the wall open to act as doors. The "roof" can also be covered with lattice to support vines.

After the arbor has been built, plant flowering vines around the perimeter, centring them on each panel. The vines can be encouraged to climb by weaving them through the lattice. It will take at least two growing seasons for them to cover the arbor.

Patios, decks and balconies

By adding trellis panels to the sides of a patio or deck you can create shading or block unwanted views. (See Garden Trellis on pages 118–119 for instructions on building a trellis.)

If it is not possible to plant vines in flower beds, use large pots for annual vines such as morning glory, thumbergia or sweet pea, which will cover considerable areas in a few weeks. Just remember that these vines will consume hefty amounts of water and soluble fertilizer.

How to grow them

By their nature, vines are vigorous and need little care. They do best in soil that has been well amended with peat moss and manure or compost. Fertilizers should be in a 1-2-1 or 1-2-2 ratio (e.g., water soluble 15-30-15), so that flower and root development is encouraged. Usually one feeding in early spring and another in early summer, with granular fertilizer, are adequate for those planted in ground beds. Water-soluble fertilizers for container-grown vines should be used every fifth watering. Prune your perennial vines every spring. Check with your local nursery for specific pruning instructions for each type of vine.

Popular vines

Some suggestions for vines: for non-flowering vines that are self-adhering try Boston ivy and English ivy or a non-self-adhering vine such as Virginia creeper. For flowering vines that are self-adhering try climbing hydrangea and trumpet vine or non-self-adhering flowering vines such as morning glory, climbing roses, clematis and wisteria.

INDEX

A

Arbors, 90, 94, 96, 111, 123
Architectural Brackets, 15

B

Balconies, 89, 115, *see also Decks, Porches and Roof Decks*
Bathrooms, 58–79
Bedrooms, 58–79
Botanical Prints, 12, 60, 61
   PROJECT
     Bloomin' Beautiful (cushions), 72

C

Candles, 42, 45, 106, 111, 112–113, 115
   PROJECTS
     Glass Acts (hurricane lamps), 121
     Lemon Candle Holders, 55
     Lighten Up (candle shades), 53
Carpentry
   PROJECTS
     Lattice Leaf (headboard), 70
     Picket Line (headboard), 71
     Garden Trellis, 118–119
     Picnic Table Perk Up, 120
     Rustic Garden Bench, 99–101
     Window Box, 102–103
Carpets, 24, 25, 30, 31, 68, 69, 115
Centrepieces, 42, 44, 46, 106, 108, 112–113, 114
   PROJECTS
     Basket Case (flower container), 50
     Lemon Centrepiece, 55
Chairs
   PROJECTS
     Muskoka Chair Makeover (deck chair), 98
     Painting a New Canvas (deck chair), 98
Chandeliers, 10–11, 44, 46, 106
Container Plants, 14, 15, 16, 85, 86–87, 90, 92, 93, 94–95, 96, 110
   PROJECTS
     Container Gardening (summertime and year-round), 104–105
     Wall Hanging (flower basket), 117
     Window Box, 102–103
Curtains, *see also Windows*
   PROJECTS
     No-Sew Billowy Curtains, 75
     Sheer Genius, 35
     Window Dressing, 78
Cushions, 16–17, 28–29, 30, 31, 49, 88, 108, 111
   PROJECTS
     Bloomin' Beautiful, 72
     Material Gains, 36
     Snappy Scrap Cushions, 39

D

Decks, 84, 85, 88, 94, 97, 104, 110, 114, *see also Balconies, Porches and Roof Decks*
Découpage
   PROJECTS
     Flower-Power Windows (curtain rods), 77
     Hang Ups (plates), 40
Dining Alfresco, 107–123
Dining Rooms, 42–57

E

Entrances, 12–21

F

Fabrics, 22, 30, 31, 36, 39, 49, 60, 61, 63, 114, 115, *see also Sewing Projects*
   PROJECTS
     Cover Up (fabric-covered storage box), 77
     Floored with Fabulous Fabric, 78–79
     Tray Chic (fabric-covered tray), 73
Flea-Market Fix-ups, cabinet, 15 chandelier, 10–11
Floors, 14, 15, 16, 22, 48, 115
   see also Sisal Carpet

PROJECTS
    Floored with Fabulous Fabric, 78–79
    On the Floor Front, 54
Flowers and Plants
    PROJECTS
        Armchair Farming, 41
        Basket Case, 50
        Blossoming Bulbs, 32–33
        Container Gardening, 104–105
        Fenced In, 51
        Fragrant Potpourri, 18–19
        Good Chemistry, 37
        Herb Appeal, 51
        Pansy Balls, 20
        Vines Grow Up, 122–123
Fresh-Air Living, 82–105

G

Going out for Dinner, 106–123

H

Headboards
    PROJECTS
        Lattice Leaf, 70
        Picket Line, 71

I

Indoor Rooms, 10–79

K

Kitchens, 42–57

L

Lamps, 10–11, 80–81
    PROJECT
        Gilded Shade, 38
Living Rooms, 22–41

O

Outdoor Rooms, 80–123
Outdoors moves Indoors, *see also Wicker*
    birdbath table, 10–11
    birdhouse, 22
    concrete garden bench, 10–11
    Corinthian column capital
        coffee table, 26
    faux fountain, 25
    garden settee, 49
    garden urn table, 25

    gargoyle, 15
    medallion, 42–43
    settee, 14
    table, 28–29
    trellis, 64
    trestle table, 42–43

P

Porches, 83, *see also Balconies, Decks and Roof Decks*
Projects
    Armchair Farming
        (planting a crop), 41
    A Stitch in Time (framed heirloom
        embroideries), 73
    Basket Case (flower container), 50
    Blind Ambition (blinds), 39
    Bloomin' Beautiful (cushion), 72
    Blossoming Bulbs, 32–33
    Clothes Cover, 76
    Coat-Hanger Cover, 76
    Cover Up (storage box), 77
    Fenced In (planter), 51
    Fit to be Tiled (table), 34
    Floored with Fabulous Fabric, 78–79
    Flower-Power Windows (curtain
        rings), 77
    Fooled You! (trompe l'oeil), 75
    Fragrant Potpourri, 18–19
    Gilded Shade (lampshade), 38
    Glass Acts (hurricane-lamp shade
        etching), 121
    Good Chemistry (flower holders), 37
    Hang Ups (découpage), 40
    Heart-Shaped Sachets, 76
    Herb Appeal (growing herbs), 51
    Keeping Tabs (kitchen curtains), 57
    Lattice Leaf (headboard), 70
    Lemon Candle Holder, 55
    Lemon Centrepiece, 55
    Lemon Place-Name Holders, 55
    Lighten Up (candle shades), 53
    Material Gains (cushions), 36
    Muskoka Chair Makeover (deck
        chair), 98
    No-Sew Billowy Curtains, 75
    Novel Napkin Rings, 116
    On the Floor Front (floor stencil), 54
    Painting a New Canvas (deck chair), 98

Pansy Balls, 20
Picket Line (headboard), 71
Picnic Table Perk Up, 120
Rustic Garden Bench, 99–101
Serviettes with Style, 54
Sheer Genius (curtains), 35
Snappy Scrap Cushions, 39
Summertime Container Plants, 104
Switched On (switch plates), 52
Table Dressing (placemats), 56
Tray Chic, 73
Turning Over a New Leaf
   (mirror), 21
Vines Grow Up, 122–123
Wall Hanging (basket of flowers), 113
Wardrobe Wizardry, 76
Weighty Subjects (tablecloth
   weights), 117
Window Box, 102–103
Window Dressing (curtains), 78
Year-Round Container Plants, 105

R

Roof Decks, 86–87, 92, 93, 96,
   see also Balconies, Decks and Porches

S

Sewing Projects
   Bloomin' Beautiful (cushions), 72
   Clothes Covers, 76
   Coat Hanger, 76
   Keeping Tabs (kitchen curtains), 57
   Material Gains (cushions), 36
   Painting a New Canvas
     (deck chair), 98
   Sachets, 76
   Serviettes with Style, 54
   Sheer Genius (curtains), 35
   Snappy Scrap Cushions, 39
   Table Dressing (placemats), 56
   Window Dressing (curtains), 78
Sheers, *see Curtains*
Sisal carpet, 10–11, 16, 28–29, 42–43,
   66–67, *see also Floors*
Slip covers, 10–11, 24, 63
Stencils, 61
   PROJECTS
     Blind Ambition (blinds), 39
     Fit to be Tiled (table), 34

Glass Acts (hurricane lamp), 121
Muskoka Chair Makeover, 98
On the Floor Front, 54

T

Table Settings, 44, 45, 55, 106, 108–109,
   110, 111, 112–113, 114, 115
   PROJECTS
     Lemon Place-Name Holders, 55
     Novel Napkin Rings, 116
     Table Dressing (placemats) 56
Tables, 10–11, 26–27, 28–29, 42–43
   PROJECTS
     Fit to be Tiled, 34
     Picnic Table Perk Up, 120
Tablecloths, 111, 112–113, 114, 115
   PROJECT
     Weighty Subjects, 117
Topiaries, 26, 42, 68
Trellis, 64, 85, 89, 90–91, 94–95, 110
   PROJECT
     Garden Trellis, 118–119
Twig Furniture, 80–81, 86–87, 106
   PROJECT
     Rustic Garden Bench, 99–101

V

Vines, 16–17, 22, 94, 96, 110, 111
   PROJECTS
     Garden Trellis, 118–119
     Vines Grow Up, 122–123

W

Wall Hangings
   PROJECT
     A Stitch in Time, 73
     Hang Ups (découpage), 40
     Wall Hangings (flowers), 117
Wicker, 16–17, 24, 25, 28–29, 42–43,
   83, 89
Windows, 14, 42–43, *see also Curtains*
   PROJECTS
     Blind Ambition (blinds), 39
     Flower-Power Windows
       (curtains rods), 77
     Keeping Tabs (kitchen curtains), 57
     No-Sew Billowy Curtains, 75
     Sheer Genius (curtains), 35
     Window Dressing (curtains), 78